MEDICAL ERROR

'Don't be alarmed,' I said, 'I am only the
doctor.'
She took no notice. Remembering that I looked
like a man from Mars in my Portuguese
balaclava, and also remembering the hearing
aid by the side of the bed, I raised my voice,
shouting 'I'M THE DOCTOR!'
By now she was out of bed, had picked up an
ebony walking stick and was standing with her
back to the wall, ready to defend her honour.
There was silence in the room as we stood eyeing
each other. During this silence a small plaintive
voice called from the room next door, 'I'm here,
Doctor.'
I had been examining the wrong patient.

Also by Dr. Robert Clifford in Sphere Books:

JUST HERE, DOCTOR!
NOT THERE, DOCTOR!
WHAT NEXT DOCTOR?
LOOK OUT, DOCTOR!
OH DEAR, DOCTOR!
SURELY NOT, DOCTOR!
THERE YOU ARE, DOCTOR!

Oh Dear, Doctor!

DR ROBERT CLIFFORD

Illustrated by Nick Baker

SPHERE BOOKS LIMITED

A SPHERE BOOK

First published in Great Britain 1981 by
Pelham Books Ltd
Published by Sphere Books Ltd 1982
Reprinted 1986, 1988, 1989

Copyright © Robert D. Clifford 1981

Reproduced, printed and bound in Great Britain by
Cox & Wyman Ltd, Reading

Sphere Books Ltd
A Division of
Macdonald & Co (Publishers)
66/73 Shoe Lane, London EC4P 4AB
A member of Maxwell Pergamon Publishing Corporation plc

For HILDA BOOTH,

*who for nine years has typed, retyped
and retyped and retyped every single
word that I have written. Grateful thanks.*

Contents

	Prologue	9
1	Mistaken Identity	11
2	Amazing Grace	18
3	A Few Eccentrics	26
4	Fight the Good Fight	39
5	Peargate	54
6	Innocents Abroad	66
7	Home Town	79
8	Life and Death	89
9	Down on the Farm	98
10	Love Me, Love My Goat	106
11	Deserving Cases	120
12	Age and Dignity	131
13	Growing Up	138
14	Schooldays	147
15	Writers' Summer School	157
16	More Things in Heaven and Earth	170
17	But Once a Year	183
	Postscript	191

Prologue

Life is a tragedy, for we are all born eventually to die. We survive our tragedies by laughing at them.

A friend once told me that when he was under the influence of ether he dreamed he was turning over the pages of a great book, in which he knew he would find, on the last page, the meaning of life.

The pages of the book were alternately tragic and comic, and he turned page after page, his excitement growing, not only because he was approaching the answer, but because he couldn't know, until he arrived, on which side of the book the final page would be. At last it came: the universe opened up to him in a hundred words: and they were uproariously funny.

He came back to consciousness crying with laughter, remembering everything. He opened his lips to speak. It was then that the great and comic answer plunged back out of his reach.

Christopher Fry

CHAPTER 1

Mistaken Identity

I hate getting out of bed to go on a call in the middle of the night. The amount of hate is in direct proportion to the lateness of the hour and the coldness of the air outside, a subjective psychological condition not unknown to general practitioners.

I knew that it had been snowing and, as I lay snugly in bed, I willed the telephone next to me to stop ringing. Failing that, that it might be a wrong number.

My wife Pam nudged me. 'Come on,' she said. 'Answer it. It might be something urgent.'

I picked up the receiver to hear a quavering, elderly female voice ask if I could come and see her. She was a Miss Hunter. She had a pain in her chest and difficulty in breathing. She apologised for having to bring me out so far, then gave me detailed instructions on how to get there. It meant my crossing to the Up-the-Hill side of the town, followed by a journey of about four miles along small lanes to her isolated house. All I had to do then, she said, was to find the key under the flower pot by the back door, take no notice of the dog – an alsatian – and come straight upstairs.

Before I ventured out I put on every scrap of clothing I could find that did not completely stop me moving my arms and legs,

11

pulled my wellingtons over some thick rugby socks, and donned an old Portuguese knitted helmet, which was a favourite of mine.

My mother had brought the helmet back from Madeira and swore to me the Portuguese peasantry wore them all the year round, ear flaps up in the summer and down in the winter. As the helmet was made of thick, heavy, oily wool, and the worst Madeira winter is about two degrees hotter than our best English summer, I wondered whether she'd got the story right. However, the helmet was beautifully warm, just right for the English winter. Mind you, with my hat pulled right down over my ears, my scarf, my duffle coat and my gum boots, I could have passed for a man from Mars.

Snow was such a rare event in Tadchester that I never thought of buying anything like chains for the car, and my journey was hair-raising. I slipped and slid up and down roads at about ten miles an hour. Having managed to scramble up the steep main road going Up-the-Hill, going down the first dip of the crest I got over-confident and spun round in a complete circle. The snow was coming down ever thicker and I seemed to be lost in a swirling curtain of flakes.

I edged my way along the lanes as the old lady had directed, came to the cross roads she had described, stepped into the white-out with my torch and stumbled to the back door. In spite of all my clothing I was already freezing, and I was not sure whether this was the house. I lifted up a flower pot by the back door. There was a key. I hoped I had got the right house; most country cottagers kept their key under a flower pot by the door.

The key turned stiffly in the lock and the door, possibly swollen by the wet weather, was difficult to open. I had to barge it a couple of times with my shoulder.

It took only a few seconds to confirm that this was the right house. A huge black alsatian, fangs bared, leapt at me as I came into the room. I was back out of the door in a flash. Strange, when I slammed the door shut it did not seem stiff at all.

12

I prowled round the house looking for another entrance. I could see a light on upstairs. Nobody answered or came to the window when I knocked, except the alsatian which appeared, snarling, at every window I looked into. A tentative touch on the back door knob had him snarling at the handle. I had to get past him. The noise he was making was enough to wake the dead, never mind the seriously ill. Obviously the lady was not well enough to come downstairs.

Stephen Maxwell, my partner, always carried a bottle of ethyl chloride spray for use on boisterous dogs. This is a freezing anaesthetic that comes out in a jet from a container like a scent bottle. I had used it for some local anaesthetics but had gained most of my experience with it as a medical student. The spray was capable of squirting a thin stream of freezing liquid about three feet and was ideal for assessing the reaction time of female medical students. If we were able to catch a female student from behind as she was bending over a cadaver during dissection, a well-directed squirt to the bare area between the top of the stocking and the knicker leg could produce the most dramatic results.

One athletic girl student, on receipt of a direct hit, leapt, with a high-pitched shriek, clean over the dissecting table. She was immediately signed up by the Secretary of the Hospital Athletic Club to represent the hospital in the united hospitals sports. On the day she performed she came a bad eighth out of nine. The use of an ethyl chloride spray was considered as bad as doping and fixing runners, and without it she just wasn't the same.

Although I was confident of some reaction when squirting this stuff up a girl student's skirt, I was not sure of its effectiveness against a great alsatian with dripping fangs. But I was so muffled up with protective clothing that it would be difficult for him to get his teeth in anywhere, so if I was going to test its efficacy on ravening beasts, this was the time.

I struggled back to the car, opened my midwifery bag and, with blue hands, picked up the cold glass cylinder. I experienced the euphoria that toting a gun must give: 'Keep your hands in the air, Kincaid. One move and I'll drop yuh!' I would have been a lot happier if it *had* been a gun.

Boldness was my only policy. I charged the door. It crashed back on its hinges and the alsatian stood snarling at bay at the back of the room, guarding the stairs which led to my patient.

Emboldened with my phial of anaesthetic, I stared him in the face. He must have been used to that one: he stared back and lifted his lip in a silent snarl. I aimed the spray at his face. The thin jet of fluid hit him straight on the bridge of the nose, spilling into his eyes. If only we could have entered that dog for the long jump instead of our lady medical student, we would have taken away the cup.

He let out one terrified yelp and cleared the stairs from bottom to top in one tremendous leap, disappearing round the corner of the landing. As I went upstairs his head poked cautiously round the corner as if he could not believe what was happening. I only had to raise the phial and, with another yelp, he shot off to some secure hiding place.

I went through the first door I could find. There was no light on, which surprised me: I thought I had seen a light from outside. Flashing my torch on the bed, I saw an elderly, grey-haired lady, either sleeping or unconscious. There was a set of false teeth in a glass by the bed, and a hearing aid beside it, which explained why she had slept through all the din.

She looked a bit blue round the lips, so I switched on the room light, put my stethoscope on her chest and felt her pulse at the wrist. It was as if I had squirted her with the ethyl chloride. She woke with a start, screamed and struggled to get out of bed. I tried frantically to reassure her.

'Don't be alarmed,' I said, 'I am only the doctor.'

She took no notice. Remembering that I looked like a man from Mars in my Portuguese balaclava, and also remembering the hearing aid by the side of the bed, I raised my voice, shouting 'I'M THE DOCTOR!'

By now she was out of bed, had picked up an ebony walking stick and was standing with her back against the wall, ready to defend her honour.

There was silence in the room as we stood eyeing each other. During this silence a small plaintive voice called from the room next door, 'In here, Doctor.'

I had been examining the wrong patient.

There was no way of communicating with a frightened deaf lady waving an ebony walking stick, so I edged backwards to the door, hoping that the alsatian would not take advantage of the seat of my pants.

In the next room I found a frail Miss Hunter sitting up in bed, surrounded by a great white shawl, and obviously very confused by all the racket. I explained hastily, but she was too unwell to laugh. When I examined her chest, having first got rid of seven or eight grey layers of flannelette, I found the cause of her trouble. She had a trail of blistery spots coming down from high up in the middle of her back, round her side and her left breast. There was no doubt about it. She had shingles.

'How long have you been in pain like this?' I asked, now shaking with reaction from the episode of the dog and the lady in the next room.

'A good two weeks,' said Miss Hunter, 'but I couldn't sleep and I thought it would be nice to have something for the pain.'

At this point, so did I.

I fished out some pain-killing tablets and ointment from my bag, and said I would arrange for the district nurse to pop in from time to time. Nurse was a dog lover, hopefully she would have a way with alsatians.

I made my farewells and, keeping close to the wall, nipped past what turned out to be Miss Hunter's deaf sister's room, got down the stairs and out of the house without seeing the dog.

I wondered how Miss Hunter would explain it all to her deaf sister. I couldn't see the sister letting anybody into her room that night, and I envisaged her standing by the door with her walking stick, ready to let the first person entering have a good crack on the head. I hoped it was the alsatian.

I got back to the car, slithered my way home, peeled off the layers of damp clothes and jumped into bed. Pam, God bless her, had left my side of the electric blanket on. However sleepy she was, she always managed to remember to reach over and put it on for me.

'I hope it wasn't serious, darling,' she said, sleepily.

'No,' I replied. 'Just an average night call.'

* * *

I was the fourth partner in a group of five in a little Somerset town called Tadchester. Tadchester (population 6,500) stands on the estuary of the River Tad, in one of the most beautiful parts of the Somerset coast. It is a market town, with some fishing, some light industry, and a great deal of farming.

The town is split in two by the River Tad, and further split by the large hill which dominates one side of the river. The other side of the river is flat pastureland, stretching off to marshes and the sea coast. You are not just a Tadchester resident – you are strictly Up-the-Hill or Down-the-Hill. It has important social distinction: the population Down-the-Hill tends to be made up of Haves, the population Up-the-Hill tends to be the Have-nots.

16

We were the only general practice in the town, and also took care of the local hospital. The five partners each had his own area of responsibility at the hospital: Steve Maxwell, the senior partner, had a special interest in medicine; Henry Johnson, the second senior, was the surgeon; Jack Hart, the third partner, was the anaesthetist; I, as the fourth partner, was reckoned to be the expert in midwifery and was pretty good at piercing ears; and Ron Dickinson, the fifth and junior partner – an accomplished athlete who spent a great deal of his time running, jumping, swimming, sailing, water ski-ing, etc – was our ENT specialist and removed the local tonsils. We were a happy and well-balanced team.

CHAPTER 2

Amazing Grace

At the time of Miss Hunter's night call I had been living in Tadchester for about ten years. Although I was beginning to look a bit like part of the local scenery and, by virtue of being a doctor, had access to most homes and an entrée into most of society, I knew I couldn't even begin to think of myself as a 'local' until I'd been there thirty years. In spite of one decade in the town, with my hair beginning to get thinner on top and my waistline moving towards solid-citizen proportions, I was still referred to as the 'new young doctor'.

I had been a bachelor when I first arrived in Tadchester, survived the ambitions of several local ladies, and married my wife, Pam, after meeting her when holidaying with my mother in Bournemouth.

After six years in a flat Up-the-Hill, we had built a house overlooking the estuary. Thinking our family of two boys was all we were going to have, we had got our rooms worked out precisely. Jane, our daughter, was born exactly nine months after we moved. I'm sure there was a very good reason.

In our original plans we had not counted on nurseries, girls' bedrooms, etc, and the tiny study and TV room had to be knocked together to remedy this deficit. The builder said we were the only people he had ever known who started knocking walls down as soon as the house had been put up.

The birth of Jane coincided with the death of Pam's mother, Bill. Pam and her mother had been extremely close but Pam was so occupied with the new baby that frankly she just had not the time to grieve. It was one of those strange balances of Nature which can do so much to heal the wounds of tragedy.

We both loved Tadchester and had made many good friends, chief among whom were Eric and his exotic wife Zara. Eric ran the Tadchester Radio Service and was the local expert on radio and television, while his arty wife Zara, with her bizarre dresses, set the fashion for ladies' wear in the Tadchester area. She was Pam's best friend and Jane's godmother.

Other friends we spent a lot of time with, particularly the nights when we trudged through the surf dragging a seine-fishing net, were Frank and Primrose Squires, Philip and Joan Gammon and Kevin and Janice Bird – all firm friends with whom to share good times, bad times, holidays and festive occasions. The men were all active members of the local Round Table and all had widely different occupations, Frank being a surveyor, Philip a school teacher and Kevin a farm manager.

My partners and their families were friends rather than working colleagues, and what with work and social goings on we were all well qualified to fill Kipling's *Unforgiving Minute* with sixty seconds' worth of distance run.

Over my working years in Tadchester I had developed a fairly standard routine. Four mornings a week I held a surgery in the practice house. (The closing of the local colliery at Thudrock meant that we no longer had to keep open the branch surgery we kept there.) I held an evening surgery two evenings a week and had an ante-natal clinic once a week. I visited Tadchester Hospital each day, usually in the late morning. There, as well as seeing my own patients who were in hospital I was also in sole charge of the recovery ward, which housed patients recovering from operations not needing intensive treatment and some medical cases.

John Bowler, the consultant physician from Winchcombe,

who held an out-patients' clinic at Tadchester Hospital once a week, used to cheat by admitting some patients direct to this recovery ward.

The name of the ward was supposed to cover its function, that is to say, you went there to recover in quiet surroundings after major medical or surgical illnesses, but as it was a quiet ward and beds were always at a premium, John Bowler had his acute medical patients admitted directly to these beds without having qualified by being iller somewhere else in the hospital before they were allowed in.

Once a week I did a ward round with him when he was seeing his patients. John was of great use to me when, after the round over a cup of coffee in the sister's office, he would help me catch up on all the latest developments and techniques in medicine with which, as a consultant, he had to keep up to date.

Midwifery occupied a great deal of my time. There was an increasing tendency for mothers to have their confinements in hospital; more and more were being delivered at St Mary's Maternity Home, and it was rumoured that a new maternity unit was going to be built at Winchcombe and we might lose our midwifery facilities altogether. But, home or St Mary's, I had to attend all the confinements. Although, being fundamentally lazy, I would be pleased to lose the out-of-hours calls, and hours at bedsides that midwifery involved, I looked upon it as an important part of medicine. I knew from giving up anaesthetics how soon one lost one's skills in any particular procedure.

There had been some changes in the surgery staff at Tadchester since I arrived. Gladys, our senior receptionist, seemed ageless and as if she would go on for ever. She was ably supported by her second-in-command, Mary Collaston, who did the typing and any dispensing that needed to be done. Mary's husband had been the under-manager at Thudrock Colliery and he was, for a time, out of work after it closed. We feared the couple might move to another area in their search to find work. However, the husband obtained a local post in charge of personnel at the new plastics factory. As this factory expanded, so did the population of Tadchester. This necessitated the appointment of our fifth partner, Ron Dickinson.

We had a succession of young ladies to help out with reception work in the surgery. Receptionists had a fairly high casualty rate, becoming pregnant or getting married, and in about fifty per cent of cases, doing both. We had one new full-time married receptionist – Grace Hughes – whose husband worked as a mechanic at one of the Tadchester garages, and an ever-changing stream of assistant receptionists.

Working at the surgery was a plum job for any girl, not because we paid them so magnificently, but because it was an ideal place to look for a husband. What was more, if you found somebody you fancied, you could always check up on his records to see he did not suffer from any nasty disease or unpleasant hereditary trait.

Grace Hughes was a great asset to the practice. She was outrageously outspoken and could get away with absolute murder. As Gladys was getting a bit older, it was Grace who always opened the surgery in the morning. When I came in she would be opening the mail.

'Good morning, Amazing Grace,' I would say, and this would receive a typical response like: 'Morning, Dr Bob. You look a little green around the gills. You've got to cut out this night-life a bit. Too much bed and too little sleep. Give the old woman a rest.'

Grace was ribald. I used to shudder sometimes at the things she said to patients. But she never offended and had such precise judgment that most other people, not venturing nearly as far as Grace, would get into awful trouble.

Two examples of Grace's handling of people will serve to illustrate her public-relations technique:

A dignified lady patient came up to the hatch.

'What's the trouble, luv?' asked Grace.

'I am passing my water rather frequently and it is stinging,' said the woman. 'I find it difficult to hold my water, and I've tried almost everything.'

'Have you tried sticking both legs into one stocking?' said Grace as she reached for the appointment book.

Anyone who dared to ask for the Family Planning Clinic which Ron Dickinson was starting as a new venture would be asked whether they had tried holding an aspirin between their knees.

Grace was always good for a laugh. There was always almost a riot going on around her. Until you knew her well, you did not realise that she had indifferent health herself and her delightful husband, Jack, had a painful spinal condition about which he never grumbled.

'No point in complaining,' said Grace. 'Life's to be lived. And I reckon a few good laughs are worth all the pills in the world.'

She was dead right. Patients would turn up at reception down in the dumps, convinced their last hour was approaching. By the time they got to me, after a quick burst of Grace's therapy, they'd be smiling broadly and almost forgetting what they'd come for.

It would be difficult to find two people more different than Gladys and Grace, and they felt for each other the attraction of opposites.

The rather fiery, prim, austere Gladys and the warm, earthy Grace got on like a house on fire. Grace would never be ribald in front of Gladys, and although Gladys shouted at most people, she would never shout at Grace.

I would sometimes come across them on a Sunday afternoon, walking their dogs together in the park, chattering away. I would love to have eavesdropped on their conversation. Henry called them the two Gee-gees and whenever he wanted assistance or some instrument taken to his room he would shout 'Gee-gee', and either Gladys or Grace (who were both a bit frightened of him) would come running.

*   *   *

One of my older friends in Tadchester was Bob Barker who kept the secondhand bookshop at Sanford-on-Sea. It was Bob who made me realise the depth of tradition and history of Tadchester. We chatted over cups of tea in his bookshop whenever I could steal half an hour from my work. He would tell me tales of his youth and of the notable figures and events that were local history. As Bob's life spanned eight decades he was himself a part of local tradition, and through him I gained some idea of the depth and strength of it.

But it was only when he took me as his guest to the Bridge Trust dinner that I realised that however long I lived in Tadchester, however warmly accepted as a doctor, I could never ever become a native.

The Bridge Trust had been founded by a man called Bernard Harding in 1600. He had set up a charitable trust – the rent from some lands – to provide monies each year for the poor of Tadchester. He had made his money from the Newfoundland cod trade. In the seventeenth and eighteenth centuries this particular trade was a very important part of Tadchester's economics and salt cod always appeared on the menu at the Bridge Trust dinners.

Senior and more important citizens of the town were honoured by being made Trustees, there being just twelve in number. It was the equivalent of a Londoner being made a Companion of Honour.

Records showed that there had been a Bridge Trust dinner and a distribution of the 'Harding Dole' every year since 1600, excepting 1640, the year of the Great Plague, when half the population of Tadchester died. The mayor and corporation fled the town, and a merchant called Robert Friend took over as mayor, organised the distribution of food, burial of the dead, and isolation of the sick. Although most Tadchestarians probably did not know the name of the current mayor, everyone knew the name of Robert Friend, the mayor who saved the town in 1640.

Every meeting of the Bridge Trustees had been recorded in a series of huge diaries which were on display at the annual dinners. They contained the names of current trustees and the names of the beneficiaries of the Harding Dole. I looked back through some of these volumes of records, some dusty old tomes with hardly legible writing, three or four hundred years old. It was interesting to note that some of the Trustees' names reappeared, generation after generation. A Barker had been a Trustee since 1647; a Hope had been a Trustee since 1700. Hope's Stores was the largest shop in Tadchester High Street, the original shop being built in 1699. And there was a Blackmore represented at every dinner from 1600, including the dinner at which I was a guest.

I felt I was extremely honoured to be asked. Each Trustee was allowed one guest. We all wore dinner jackets, and all twenty-four of us sat round a long deal table.

There was a simple ceremony, glasses were raised in memory of Bernard Harding, salt cod was served, and the business of the Trustees discussed. The meeting had an air of permanence about it: these delightful old men, surrounded by old books, carrying on traditions that had been in existence for nearly four centuries. I would not have been surprised if Sir Walter Raleigh had walked through the door. I thought to myself that if, God willing, I lived the rest of my life in Tadchester and safely reached the age of three score and ten, I would have covered only a short span of time in relation to this town, its traditions and its fine old men who, for dozens of generations, had maintained these traditions and their charitable bequests.

I felt very humble.

CHAPTER 3

A Few Eccentrics

Tadchester had its quota of eccentric patients, and of them I seemed to get more than my share. I used to wonder what it was about me that attracted them.

One fat lady patient, Millicent Foggat, had repeated chest infections but she utterly refused to let me listen to her chest. I was allowed only to put my stethoscope on the outside of her jumper. The fact that I could hear nothing, she passed off with a little smile as irrelevant. She knew I was really wanting to see her body – all sixteen stone of it.

I once disobeyed her instructions and tried to lift the back of her jumper to put my stethoscope onto real live flesh. There was an immediate explosion. She turned round indignantly as if I had tried to rape her and yelled, 'Stop it, Doctor!'

She agreed eventually to go and have her chest x-rayed, but only on condition she kept her jumper on throughout the proceedings.

It was not the first time in my career I had been commanded to 'Stop it!' It had also happened when I was a medical student.

Once I had attained my second MB, which meant I had passed my test in anatomy and physiology, before starting on full clinical studies in the hospital, I went on what was known as a clinical introduction course.

Thirty students would be shepherded around in a group, being introduced to different aspects of hospital life and clinical teaching. We were taught how to examine a patient, or rather we were supposed to be taught: there were so many of us that only two or three of the keenest at the front ever saw or grasped what was going on.

I was secretary of the rugby club at that time and kept out of sight on the fringe of the crowd, working out who was going to play in which team on the following Saturday, where we were going to hire the coaches from, and whether the club could afford it.

We were doing a round in the surgical ward one day. I was in my usual position on the fringe when the lecturer called out, 'Hey – you at the back! Come over here and examine this breast.'

I ducked my head lower. He couldn't be wanting me. But he was. The students in front of me parted, revealing a finger pointing straight at me.

Also revealed was a large, pale-looking woman with huge pendulous breasts sitting upright like a stag at bay with thirty students crammed round her bed.

'Clifford,' said the lecturer, 'this woman complains of a lump in her breast. Come and examine it and tell us what you think about it. If you think at all, that is.'

I hadn't examined a breast before, leastways not professionally. But there had to be a first time. I stretched out some tentative fingers towards the huge breast, with all my friends crowding round expectantly. The woman eyed me mistrustfully.

I made a grab at what I thought was the lumpy area to have my fingers smacked down, accompanied by a shout of, 'Stop it, Doctor! That's enough of that!'

I was completely embarrassed, both by the woman and by my friends who broke out into disapproving mutters of 'Sexy, sexy . . .'

The lecturer had decided prudently to exit from the scene. I realised I was going to get no further with the examination, so I tracked him down. 'What did I do wrong?' I asked.

'Shouldn't manhandle them,' he said brusquely. 'And you should pay more attention.'

I never found out what was wrong with the patient. I'm ashamed to say that at the time I hoped it was something nasty.

* * *

Basil Small was another patient who didn't trust doctors. When he had to have surgery, he decided to keep the treatment as short as possible. He discharged himself from hospital two days after his hernia operation, when he was also carrying stitches in a large cut to his forehead (a burglar had knocked him out with a jemmy – it wasn't Basil's week!).

Always filthy and unwashed, Basil was reputed to have a large cache of money hidden somewhere in his derelict farmhouse. It was rumoured also that somewhere on his farm he kept his mother and sister in a chicken house. As he never welcomed visitors, and there were always about six ferocious dogs wandering about, nobody ventured to find out if the rumours were true.

Basil reluctantly called to see me about three months after his operation. I found that his two lots of stitches, being nylon, were still firmly in place. His hernia stitches now resembled dirty undergrowth. Those in his head were stuck together under several layers of dried blood, sweat and grime. He looked as if he had a horn sticking out of his forehead.

'Basil,' I said, 'do you know you are an endangered species? You must be one of the last of the unicorns.'

Basil didn't think that was funny at all. He wouldn't let me touch his stitches at this visit, but promised to come again sometime. All he had come for, this time, was a bottle of 'white medicine', and he wasn't going to hang about for anything else.

Basil was slow, but not all that slow – as I was to discover.

In that year he had sold the pheasant-shooting rights over his land to no less than three different syndicates.

Members of shooting syndicates tend to be pretty well-breeched, as was the case here, and there were terrible legal wrangles going on. Basil was summoned to appear in court.

He came to me terrified – at heart he was a simple country man – and even allowed me to remove the septic remnants of his stitches.

'I bain't going to court, Doctor,' he said. 'I'd ruther shoot miself. Can you fix it?'

I believe he would have shot himself if the case had proceeded, so I wrote endless letters, made dozens of telephone calls and finally managed to get the whole thing dropped.

Basil came in to thank me, as dirty as usual and leaving one of his mongrel dogs tied to the post outside the surgery.

'Thank 'ee, Doctor,' he said. 'You're a gentleman. I bain't much good with these 'ere money things.'

'You could have fooled me,' I said. 'Anybody who can sell something three times can't be all that daft. Just one word of advice: if you *are* going to have problems with people, try to avoid having them with people who have plenty of money.'

I told Steve Basil's story at coffee one morning.

Steve laughed. 'As we grow older', he said, 'it is inevitable that our faculties begin to deteriorate. But the very last faculty of all to go is the one that's concerned with money.

'Don't feel too sorry for dirty old Basil Small, the poor old man you have spent so much time and trouble on – he's probably worth about a quarter of a million pounds!'

*   *   *

Another of Tadchester's eccentrics – if absolute regularity of habit can be called eccentricity – was Arnold Bishop, a bachelor in middle age.

His Saturdays followed the same pattern to the minute: a perambulation around Tadchester covered market, then around the museum, followed by a crawl around the same four pubs. He always spent his holidays in the same hotel in Libya every year. He liked neither Libya nor the hotel, but at least he knew what he didn't like.

So I was surprised to learn that he had taken up astronomy in a big way, and was installing a telescope in his tiny attic flat.

'Nothing more natural, my dear chap,' he said. 'I am, as you know, a creature of habit. And there is nothing so regular as the stars in their courses. In an uncertain world it is a great comfort to observe the unchanging beauty of the heavenly bodies.'

A month later, after a discreet call from a plain-clothes policeman, Arnold sold his telescope. He had been observing heavenly bodies all right, but these were changing ones – changing their clothes in the nurses' home.

Intrigued by strange reflections from Arnold's flat one moonlit night, a nurse had used a pair of binoculars. They revealed Arnold in his darkened attic room, one eye glued to the telescope and the telescope trained directly on the windows of the nurses' home.

The story soon got around Tadchester and it took Arnold some time to live it down. The thing that seemed to bother him, however, was that his actions would seem to be some kind of deviation from the norm, something out of keeping with his usual routines.

'Nothing of the kind, old boy,' he said. 'It has always been my ambition to become a dirty old man. And this seemed a perfectly logical step in the process . . .'

*　　　*　　　*

Among my patients in Tadchester were many who did not believe in conventional medicine.

Some had explored everything that conventional medicine had to offer and were still not free of their particular malady. Others had been given a hopeless prognosis, others were just plain misfits. All went off and visited various fringe areas of medicine. Some of the fringe practitioners were well established, and some were way beyond the fringe.

I have never been able to believe, for instance, that people with inoperable diseases can go to the Far East and have tumours removed without operation and without any residual scars; much as I'd like to believe it.

A larger group than those who deserted conventional medicine were those who used it as a last resort. I once had a call from a religious sect who asked me if I would pop in and leave a death certificate for one of their members. They didn't want me to look at him. One of their beliefs was in everlasting life and they didn't want anybody as square as a general practitioner to see one of their failures.

I never minded anybody having any course of treatment that got him better, providing (a) the patient was adequately investigated and (b) he wasn't going off on some course of therapy that delayed prompt treatment by conventional methods.

One patient came to see me after his pet spinal manipulator had failed to improve the pain in his back. An x-ray showed that his spine was riddled with cancer. Although I couldn't change the course of events at this stage, I could give him something for his pain, rather than have it aggravated by unnecessary spinal manoeuvres.

31

Mind you, I have always believed that even the most conventional doctor has to be part witch doctor. The relationship between doctor and patient is terribly important, and if you really believed that the doctor who was looking after you could get you better, then you were a long way towards recovery. Similarly, I expect, if you believed that your witch doctor could lower your blood pressure by slapping you across the bottom with some stinging nettles, there would be a good chance that your blood pressure would come down if he did so.

I had read of witch doctors, herbalists and various other people coming in to save the day when conventional medicine had failed, but I didn't have any first-hand acquaintance with this until Mr. Nin, a Malaysian diplomat, bought a holiday cottage at Tadchester. Over the years he became a close friend.

Among Mr. Nin's duties was the care of Malaysian students in Britain and the arranging of medical care and treatment for senior diplomats and royalty, both in Malaysia and over here.

Mr. Nin, a small, lightly tanned man with a perpetual smile, was only too pleased to talk about unorthodox medicine as practised at home.

He told me of one senior Malaysian official who came over to Britain with a heart condition, and was told he only had a few months to live. He went back to Malaysia, saw the local Bomo (witch doctor) and was given some herbs. Twenty years later he was still happily running around and full of beans.

'Fine,' I said, 'but this is another of those second-hand stories. What have you experienced yourself?'

He smiled his inscrutable oriental smile and told me of his earliest encounter with a Bomo, which happened when he was a small boy and his sister was ill. He didn't know what the illness was, but she had been ill for a very long time and everybody assumed that she was going to die. The doctor had come and gone and all hope had been given up.

The local Bomo was called in. Straightaway he put her into a trance. She stayed in the trance for three days then sat up in bed and started to speak fluently in Malay, English, Chinese and French.

32

That would have been amazing enough, except that before the trance she spoke only Malay.

She broke off in the middle of the multi-lingual discourse to shout, 'Look out! There's a tiger downstairs!'

The house they lived in was built on stilts. Mr. Nin and the family went out onto the verandah and looked down. There, beneath the stilts, was a large tiger.

This event marked the beginning of the girl's full recovery.

Mr. Nin offered no explanation. He merely accepted it as something that had happened.

He was a social friend, rather than a medical one, and was very pleasant and easy to talk to. But one day he came to see me about his health. He wondered whether he had a touch of malaria. I did some blood tests and reassured him they were negative.

When I asked had he had malaria before, he smiled and said yes, he had had it as a teenager. He had been very, very ill and he was not responding to the normal drugs. Mr. Nin was so ill, apparently, that he wasn't taking fluid, hadn't opened his bowels for ten days and was running a high fever. The Bomo was called in but could effect no improvement.

'There is nothing else for it,' said Mr. Nin's mother. 'We will have to send for the Sensen.'

(The Sensen, apparently, was a Chinese witch doctor, whether mainland Chinese or Malayan Chinese I never discovered.)

The Sensen came, took one look at Mr. Nin, then fished in his bag. He brought out a small bottle of dirty water and told him to drink it. He then pulled out a tin can, fixed it to the light fixture above Mr. Nin's head, and filled it with water.

The tin had a small hole in the bottom. As Mr. Nin lay in bed, water dropped on his forehead. It fell drop by drop (much as I'd imagine the Chinese water torture).

That night Mr. Nin had a tremendous evacuation of his bowels. When he woke up in the morning his temperature was gone, and he was completely better.

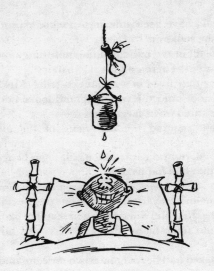

'I have no explanation for it,' he told me. 'All I can do is vouch for the truth.'

What splendid treatment, I thought. I had a number of patients I should like to have pinned to the bed with water continually drip, drip, dripping onto their heads. I am sure most of the awkward ones would be cured permanently by this treatment. The big worry would be if one of them didn't deserve it ...

* * *

Some patients have a particular quality of cheerfulness whatever circumstances they might be in. Miss Gill, an old lady who was bedridden for forty-seven years, had it. She led a happy and successful life within the four walls of her bedroom.

Reg Dawkins, a patient with a complicated disease – pseudo-muscular dystrophy of the limb-girdle type – had it to excess. His condition meant that from his waist upwards his body worked, and from his waist downwards it worked. Unhappily the connections between the upper and lower halves didn't and he was confined to a wheel chair.

I used to go to him to be cheered up, and at least once a fort-night would pop in to see Reg and his wife Mary for a chat, and a glass of their home-made wine.

From time to time he would have to go into hospital where, in spite of his disability, he was as good as a blood transfusion to the patients whose beds lay close to his.

Mary and Reg were regularly visited at home by a couple whose son, severely injured and depressed after a car accident, had the good fortune to be in bed next to Reg. They attributed their son's subsequent recovery, and regaining of the will to live, solely to Reg's cheerful encouragement and presence.

'All I did was to act daft,' said Reg. 'Once, for instance, I rattled my pills around my mouth and made choking sounds. I shouted for the male charge-nurse.

'"What's the matter?" he said.

'"My sleeping pills have gone down the wrong way, and one of my lungs has gone to sleep."

'"Silly bugger," said the charge-nurse.'

*　　*　　*

A third cheerful patient and perhaps the most endearing of all, was a doctor colleague, Dr. Jacqueline Dean.

Jackie had been a brilliant student, taking an honours degree in chemistry, before taking up medicine, then winning most of the hospital prizes as a medical student. She was an accomplished horsewoman and rode to hounds. She had the makings of a brilliant surgeon, and was climbing the ladder as a plastic surgeon when a severe debilitating illness forced her to give up medicine. Eventually, apart from a weekly trip round the garden with the physiotherapist, she was confined to bed.

Jackie was almost a medical museum, you name it she had it. She had bone trouble, bowel trouble, blood trouble, liver trouble and had been examined and operated on at various times by the finest specialists in the land.

She reached a relatively stable state, but was very limited in what she could do. She was looked after by her sister, who was of much the same ilk as Jackie, with weekly visits from the district nurse and physiotherapist.

Jackie was always cheerful and regaled me with stories of her days as a medical student. She was one of the first female students to enter medical school, when it became compulsory for these male chauvinistic establishments to have at least ten per cent of females in their yearly intake.

The ratio of boys to girls was about fifty to one and Jackie had a rough time. The idea of girl medical students was not a popular one: the ungentlemanly men were rude to them, propositioned them openly, and made life as difficult as they could.

'There has only been one man in my life,' said Jackie, 'and that's John Wayne. Unfortunately I've had to conduct my romance via the television and cinema screen – but if you could ever get him up into my room here, I would eat him.'

When Jackie qualified and became a house surgeon things changed very little. She literally had to fight for survival.

'There was this pesty Australian registrar,' she said. 'He thought I was a perk of the job, and should come up to his room for instructions, not all of them medical. Finally, one evening I said to him, "Having you put your hand down my blouse is not part of my duties," and I punched him on the nose. He never troubled me again.'

Even in the operating theatre, Jackie could hold her own. On being sworn at by one famous consultant surgeon, she picked up a bloodstained swab, scored a direct hit on his face mask and walked out of the theatre.

Her final disillusionment with men was when another consultant, a man she had previously admired, suggested after a particularly arduous operating session that they go for a spin in his car.

They drove out to some beautiful woodland country, stopped the car and got out. Whereupon the consultant immediately tried to press her against the nearest fir.

'I'm afraid,' said Jackie as she fought off his embrace, 'that you're barking up the wrong tree.'

'How would it have been,' I asked, 'if it had been John Wayne with you up there in the wood?'

'Fine,' replied Jackie with a twinkle in her eye, 'but only if he wasn't wearing his spurs . . .'

*　　*　　*

My eccentrics came in all shapes and sizes, as proven by Gladys and Ralph Dimond who kept a small greengrocery shop at Sanford-on-Sea, three doors away from Bob Barker's secondhand bookshop.

They certainly were an odd-looking couple. Gladys, who weighed in at about fifteen and a half stone, was twice the size of Ralph who was a diminutive seven stone. Their oddness was accentuated by the fact that they both always wore bowler hats. I never knew why, but thought it was in an effort to keep up with the Joneses: their nextdoor neighbour, Jones the butcher, always wore a striped apron and straw boater.

From behind, Ralph and Gladys looked exactly like Laurel and Hardy. In addition to the bowler hats, Gladys insisted that they both wore cumbersome boiler suits.

The chance of seeing them walking together was rare, however. Gladys was hardly ever seen moving at all. From early morning to closing time she sat on a high stool behind the till, shouting instructions to Ralph. Poor Ralph was kept leaping about all day with sacks of potatoes, crates of oranges and apples, swedes, turnips and tomatoes and all the other ingredients of their trade. He was a sort of greengrocer's Jimmy Wild – a flyweight, daring anything of any weight to last three rounds with him.

I wondered how he managed it: he didn't look strong enough to lift a banana skin.

The pace eventually told on him. He came to my surgery one day, after a particularly fierce battle with some sacks of potatoes.

'Doctor,' he said, 'I've a lump down below. Do you think I've got a hernia?'

I examined him. 'Yes, Ralph,' I said, 'your diagnosis is

right. I'm afraid you are going to need an operation.'

'Will the operation affect my sex life?' queried Ralph.

'No,' I replied. 'Your performance might even be better. Anyway, the operation certainly won't reduce it.'

'OH DEAR, DOCTOR!' said Ralph. 'All that sort of thing had settled down. I hope the operation isn't going to start it up again.'

CHAPTER 4

Fight
the Good Fight

One of the most satisfying aspects of general practice is when a straightforward case (if there is such a thing) comes to a straightforward and reassuring end. A good example was George Ford.

George Ford staggered into my surgery, clutching his chest.

'I nearly had to break my record this time, Doc,' he said. 'There's something bad going on. I think I've had a heart attack or got pleurisy or something.'

It had been George's proud boast that in fifty years he had never had to send for a doctor. He certainly did not look well on this occasion. He was breathless, with rapid, shallow breathing, and in obvious pain.

'What has been happening to you, George?' I asked.

'I was perfectly well yesterday,' he said. 'I helped my neighbour put up some fencing. I was as fit as a flea, lifting the fencing posts around and swinging a sledge hammer. Haven't felt so fit for years. When I woke this morning,' he said, 'every time I took a breath, I got this pain in my chest and I could hardly breathe. Is it serious, Doc?'

'Take your shirt off, George,' I said. 'We'll have a look.'

I examined him carefully. His blood pressure and heart were

39

normal. Listening to his chest, although his breathing was rapid, both lungs appeared to have nothing wrong with them.

'Well, George,' I said, 'your heart and chest are clear. Let's have a look at the rest of you.'

I poked around in the spaces between his ribs with my finger, then I hit a point when George shouted, 'You've got it, Doc. That's the spot.' Between George's ribs I located a very tender spot which made him jump when I pressed it.

'The diagnosis is simple,' I said. 'Nothing terrible has happened. What is troubling you is the result of your fencing activities yesterday. You have torn a muscle between the ribs and every time you take a breath it stretches and causes you pain. The medical name for this condition is called intercostal myalgia, not that that will be of any help to you, but it is as painful as breaking a rib. To be absolutely certain, we ought to get your chest x-rayed, but I am pretty sure of my diagnosis. I am going to give you some simple pain relievers that will ease it, but it may take two or three weeks for it to go completely. You must avoid heavy lifting during that time, and try not to laugh or sneeze too much.'

George's x-ray was quite clear, as I thought it would be.

I found that he had worried all the time until he heard his x-ray result and, although still in pain, he immediately felt better.

So often a negative result like a normal chest x-ray makes patients improve rapidly.

I warned George that there are many conditions that can cause chest pain. Some are connected with bones and muscles, like intercostal myalgia; others are connected with the heart or with the lungs; even indigestion can give pain in the chest. I emphasised that if he should ever again get a sudden attack of pain in the chest, particularly if he found breathing difficult, he mustn't make his own diagnosis, he mustn't struggle to the surgery to see me, he must break his golden rule and ask me to come and see him wherever he was.

George, who was a carpenter, had to have ten days off work. He came to see me, smiling, for his signing-off medical certificate to start work again.

He said, grinning, 'I told my mates at work I was stabbed in the chest, fencing, Doc.

'They think I'm training secretly for the Olympic Games.'

*　　　*　　　*

Cases with an ending as happy as George's are rare. Among the routine cases that came to the surgery I usually had at least one fight on my hands coping with serious illness. Sometimes the fight was literally between life and death.

I was called one weekend to the house of a naval commander. He was obviously well-to-do: there was a substantial house, stables, and lawns running down to the River Tad.

He either had a wealthy wife, or had inherited money. Properties of that size were not come by on a commander's pay.

His message on the telephone was terse and irritating.

'I want you to come round straight away and do something about my wife – I am not going to put up with this any longer.'

Then he slammed the phone down. In the background I thought I could hear breaking crockery.

I don't like being spoken to like that. I was not one of his midshipmen.

The commander and his wife were patients of Jack Hart. I remembered Jack saying something about the wife having a psychiatric problem, but I couldn't recall the details.

I drove up the immaculately kept drive and rang the door bell.

The commander's voice shouted through the window near the door, 'Let yourself in the back door, Doctor. I daren't let go of this bitch.'

I walked round the back, in through a kitchen filled with smashed crockery, and through to a front lounge to confront a man whom I assumed was the commander. He was forcibly holding, face-down on the settee, a smartly dressed attractive-looking woman whom I took to be about thirty-five.

As I came into the room she twisted her head round and, in a

41

calm controlled voice, said:

'Thank God you've come, Doctor – see what this brute is doing to me.'

'Don't take any notice of her, Doctor,' said the commander. 'She tried to have a go at me with a knife – I want her out of here and back into hospital, but quick. Have you seen what she's done to the kitchen?'

I assumed from his 'back into hospital, quick' that something like this had happened before.

'This is silly,' said the wife in her continued calm, well-modulated voice. 'I was a bit upset, and smashed a few things in the kitchen, what woman doesn't? He was so angry I thought he was going to hit me, so I just held a knife to defend myself.

'Please will you make him let go of me so we can sit up and talk, calmly. I am afraid it's my husband who needs treatment.'

I was beginning to side with the wife; I hate violence. Here was this hulking man using physical force on her. Perhaps she had to defend herself. Anyway, I didn't like the way he had spoken to me on the telephone.

'Let your wife sit up,' I said.

'No,' he replied.

'Look,' I said, 'you have dragged me out on a Saturday afternoon – if you don't do as I say, then I shall just go and leave you to it.'

The commander reluctantly stood up, adjusting his suit that he had rumpled in the struggle.

His wife swung her legs down so she was sitting on the settee, took a compact out of her handbag, powdered her nose, touched up her hair, then smiled at me and said, 'Thank you, Doctor. It is nice to know that there is one gentleman in the house.'

I had a better look at her now: she really was extremely smart and very good looking. Poor thing, being married to such a husband.

The commander was pacing up and down. 'Doctor,' he said,

'do you realise I had to keep her tied up all last night?

'I insist that you send her to hospital.'

At the mention of the word hospital the wife was off the settee like a cat. A well-directed kick to the crotch had the commander down, and I was just in time to save him from a stiletto heel being driven into his skull.

I wrestled the shoe away and sat astride the wife, pinning her hands to the floor. She giggled, 'Do you do this often Doctor? Thank goodness I have at last managed to give that bastard what he deserves. Couldn't we sit somewhere comfortable?'

Still keeping a close grip on her I got up and led her to the settee. We sat facing each other with me still gripping her wrists.

'This is cosy, Doctor,' she said, smiling.

I couldn't help liking her, and the commander did look such an idiot groaning on the floor clutching his recently injured area.

'Look here,' said the wife, 'I've done my bit of protesting, I promise to behave now. I'll do whatever you suggest, but please could I have a cigarette and, much as I like you holding me, you are squeezing my wrists rather tightly.'

Thinking I was in control of the situation, I let go of her.

She sat rubbing her wrists thoughtfully for a minute, looked into my eyes, smiled – then punched me smack in the mouth.

I was just in time to stop her getting out of the window. 'Bloody pig!' she said. 'Didn't they tell you not to trust me?'

Suddenly I was completely on the commander's side.

We took it in turns to restrain her, whilst I made arrangements for a duly authorised officer to come. As GP I could not compulsorily order a patient to be admitted to hospital without the consent of a duly authorised officer; it was his job to do the actual committing. Our two regular officers were off duty, and I had to bring one in from some way away.

All the time we were holding the commander's wife she was sweet reasonableness. She had lost her battle, so would we let go of her?

Please could she have a cigarette?

She wanted to go to the toilet.

There was nothing doing. We sat firmly holding her on the settee.

I did not know the duly authorised officer who eventually arrived – he was younger than usual. Duly authorised officers who were well versed in general and mental nursing were rarely under the age of forty.

I watched this young man confidently go through the routine I had been through myself.

'You can release her now I'm here,' he said.

'Thank you, sir,' said the commander's wife. 'These two men are pigs – all I asked was to go and fetch my cigarettes.'

Like an attentive courtier the officer snapped open a cigarette case, and followed it up with a snappy lighter.

The commander's wife gave him her special intimate smile, drew deeply on her cigarette and blew the smoke out through her nose. Calm, collected, poised; as if she was a small island of sanity in a sea of idiots.

The officer was definitely on her side.

'Now what's all this about, Doctor?' said the officer. 'I was called urgently and I have come a very long way. So far I can see no reason for either the urgency or the need for my journey.'

The commander's wife literally beamed at her new champion.

I said, 'I must ask for an order for this lady for her immediate admission to hospital.'

As I said the word hospital, I was just able to duck in time to prevent the commander's wife sticking her lighted cigarette into my left eye.

'Now, my dear,' said the officer, as he put out a hand to restrain her. 'Remove your hand,' said the commander's wife ominously.

The officer had hardly mouthed his next 'Now, my dear', when the commander's wife put her head forward, sank her teeth into his thumb, jumped over the back of the settee, and was out through the open window and away.

'Quick, all outside,' said the commander. 'If we don't catch her she will be gone for days.'

'But my thumb is bleeding,' wailed the officer. 'Look, Doctor. Look at my thumb.'

I followed the commander outside. We scoured the grounds for half an hour, eventually finding his wife behind a laurel bush, quite close to the house, as if she wanted to be caught.

The duly authorised officer was still fussing about his thumb, now wrapped in a large handkerchief, when we returned.

He insisted that I gave him an anti-tetanus injection before he got on with formally committing the commander's wife to hospital.

Eventually a hospital car arrived and the commander's wife, accompanied by a very wary mental officer, drove away.

I sat for a while with the commander. 'The trouble is,' he said, 'in two weeks she will be practically running the hospital, and in a further two weeks they will send her home and it will

45

start all over again.

'She used to be such a fine gel. Nobody seems to be able to help, or even tell me what it is.'

I felt terribly sorry for him as I left him sitting alone in his lovely house with its smashed kitchen. Poor chap, there are some types of mental illness that, as yet, we do not know how to cope with.

I subscribe to the belief that some mental conditions could be chemical or biochemical in origin and that, some day, simple remedies will be found. I take heart in the fact that disorders of the thyroid gland, too much and too little, were thought of as mental disorders until the working of the thyroid gland was understood and controlled.

I arrived home late, tired and worn; I had spent nearly seven hours all told at the commander's.

'Have you had an awful time?' Pam asked.

'Let's say it's been a struggle,' I replied.

*   *   *

But it wasn't only doctors who had to fight for a living.

John Denton, the local river bailiff, had a lot of trouble with professional poachers, especially during late spring and early summer.

They would come in small gangs by night, in cars or trucks, from as far away as London or Birmingham, armed with nets, snares, fish spears, searchlights, poison and sometimes explosives. For them it was strictly a commercial operation – they could bag dozens of salmon inside a few hours – and they had no scruples about clubbing down any bailiff or policeman who came across them.

Late one night in spring, John ran into such a gang. The first I knew of it was a phone call in the early hours.

'Bob, lad, would you mind coming out to the cottage? I've run into some villains and they've given me a fair old working over. They've hurt Biddy as well; she's in a worse state than I am, poor little sod.'

46

Biddy was John's collie – a soft-eyed, gentle bitch who went everywhere with him.

'What's the damage, do you think?' I asked.

'Couple of cracked ribs, Bob. And a broken leg.'

'God,' I said. 'I'll be right over. Make yourself comfortable. And don't move!'

I drove to the cottage as fast as I could and screeched to a stop outside the garden gate. The front door opened and there stood John, clutching his chest.

'What the hell are you playing at, John?' I yelled as I lugged out my bag. 'You shouldn't be moving with a broken leg!'

'Sorry, Bob,' he said. 'I realised as soon as I put the phone down. I've got the cracked ribs; Biddy's got the broken leg. Could you see to her first? I've phoned the vet, but he's out at a farm on an emergency.'

'OK,' I said. 'I'll treat Biddy first. But before that I'll give you a quick once-over just to make sure there are no complications setting in.'

'Complications? Such as what?'

'Such as death. Now stand there and shut up.'

Under the living-room light, John looked a lot worse than he had at the front door. He had caked blood on his scalp, a split lip and a red, green and purple eye. When he took off his shirt there was more: quite extensive bruising around the ribs and abdomen. ('Abdomen' is the polite medical term for what ballooned out over John's trousers when he took his shirt off.)

The ribs on his left side were obviously painful and almost certainly damaged. But the kidneys seemed to have missed the worst of the onslaught. John would live all right. He could be left safely for a while to sit in the armchair and kill the pain with a bottle of Scotch. Biddy, I wasn't so sure about.

'Tell me what happened, John,' I said. 'It will help me to look after Biddy.'

'I got word at the last knockings in the pub that there were villains on the river,' said John. 'Real villains. Offcomers.

'It would have been sensible to go through the proper channels – ring the police and all that – but round here you know

47

what happens: what the hell could Charlie Willis do that I couldn't?'

Police Constable Charles Redvers Willis was the local equivalent of the Flying Squad. He was getting on and creaking a bit and his pushbike wasn't much better.

'It was no use swearing in a posse at the Tadchester Arms, either. You should have seen the state of 'em. I'd have left half of 'em in the river. So, daft-like – and I admit I'd had a few – I decided to sort it out myself.'

'And?'

'They sorted me out. I never learn. There were five or six of 'em.'

'Would you recognise them again?'

'Two of 'em I would. One's got my knuckle prints right across his nose. And he's the one that kicked Biddy. I'd seen to him when his mate came up behind and dropped me. "Broken Nose" got up and the pair of 'em put the boot in. That's when Biddy came in like a good 'un, but that bastard Broken Nose kicked her twice, once in the leg and then in the belly. Then they ran off.

'If it hadn't been for Biddy, they might very well have done for me. She was carrying, you know. And she dropped her pups where she lay. Six of 'em. She was nowhere near full term, thank God, but it was bad enough. I wiped her down, best I could, then carried her home. And that's when I rang you. I've rung the police since. Happen they might pick the bastards up.'

I looked at Biddy and felt gently along her smashed hind leg. When my fingers reached the break, it obviously hurt. But she uttered no more than a stifled whimper and let me carry on. Both back legs were caked with dried blood and mucus from the loss of the pups.

I am slow to come to the boil. In my job you have to be. But I knew what I would have done if the poachers were brought before me at that moment; the thought was quite frightening.

I cleaned Biddy's hindquarters and then set the leg in the splints and pads I'd brought for John. I prided myself that I'd done a good job, particularly on a patient who could not speak and whose indications of pain were muted because she knew I was doing my clumsy best. She would be as comfortable as I could make her until Andrew Thomas, the vet, could call round.

Biddy's trusting eyes reinforced my respect for vets. They are called out to attend to everything from an egg-bound budgie to a miscarrying cow, and have to do their job entirely without the question-and-answer routine which gives general practitioners the vital clues to what might be wrong.

Doctors deal with one species. Vets deal with dozens, from one end of the evolutionary scale to the other. What they do is backed by a very thorough training, but in the last analysis they have to rely on a certain amount of instinct and an ability to think themselves into the mind of the animal they are treating. It is a sensitivity I would be proud to own.

After treating Biddy, I cleaned and dressed John's cuts and bruises, strapped up his ribs and put his left arm in a sling to restrict potentially painful movement. After a Scotch and a few reassuring words for John, I drove back home to bed and collapsed into merciful sleep.

I was off duty the next day, and made the most of it by sleeping late. About noon the bedside telephone extension rang. Pam intercepted the call downstairs then came up to the bedroom. 'I'm sorry, darling, it's the police, I couldn't put them off.'

I picked up the telephone.

'Dr Clifford? Inspector Downing here, Tadchester Constabulary. I'd be grateful if you could call round to the station to attend to a casualty. Broken collar bone, I think. I understand you may be familiar with the background: John Denton and the poachers he ran into last night.'

'I'll be round straightaway,' I said. 'But how did John come to break a collar bone?'

'He didn't. Somebody else did. You'll understand when you get here.'

Muttering uncomplimentary things about John, I pulled on

my clothes, didn't bother to wash, shave, or even clean my teeth, and drove blearily to what was known familiarly as the Tadchester Nick.

'Thanks for coming so promptly, Doctor,' said the Inspector. 'The patient is in here.'

He led me down a corridor to one of a row of cells. Inside sat a large, unappetising character with a strip of sticking plaster across his nose and a left arm supported by a regulation first-aid sling.

'We strapped him up as best we could,' said the Inspector. 'But I'd be happier if he had some professional attention.'

'I think I know what happened,' I said. 'Where's John?'

'In the next cell until he cools down. You can see him when you've finished.'

I strapped up the collar bone and immobilised the arm – almost unnecessarily, since the constable who had administered first aid obviously knew what he was doing. The Inspector took me into the interview room to tell me the full story.

'After John had telephoned last night, we put the word out to the County lads. They're a bit more mobile than we are; they've got cars that work. As it happened, they'd already stopped a van and found it full of fish-snatching gear and suspicious-looking characters. Including one whose nose had come into contact with something large and heavy.'

'Such as John's fist?'

'Such as John's fist. Anyway, they brought the whole kit and caboodle down here and this morning we got John over for an identification parade. I suppose you get that feeling now and again, that you wished you'd never got out of bed?'

'Often,' I said. 'And this sounds like being another time.'

It had been a big identification parade. There were five suspects altogether, and the police had a job to muster enough villainous-looking Tadchester residents to swell the ranks. But with the help of six or so hung-over holidaymakers, some hung-over drunks who had been held overnight, and a few ex-miners from Thudrock, they managed it.

John was brought in as the only witness.

'If you recognise anyone, place your hand on his shoulder,' said the Inspector.

'My hand?' said John.

'Your hand,' said the Inspector.

'On his shoulder?' said John.

'On his shoulder,' said the Inspector.

'Right,' said John.

Walking stiffly and painfully, John approached a large man with a strip of sticking plaster across his nose. Other large men in the parade had also been decorated with sticking plaster, but John never forgot a face. Especially one he had seen so recently and had so much cause to remember.

He reached the man, raised his right hand and smashed the palm into the man's left shoulder. The man crashed back against the wall.

'That's for Biddy,' said John. Apparently so quietly and coldly that it sent a shiver up the spine of even the hardened Inspector.

'And that's for her pups,' said John, smashing his giant hand again into the man's shoulder as he rebounded from the wall.

The man finished up writhing on the floor, his collar bone smashed, and John stepped back.

'Right lads,' he said to the startled policemen, for whom everything had happened too quickly for them to move in. 'That's all the identifying I'm doing. You can take me away now – only don't put me in the same cell as that bloody swine. Not if you want two for court in the morning.'

'We had to tell the poacher that he was perfectly entitled to prefer charges for assault against John,' said Inspector Downing. 'But once he realised what he'd done to the dog, he understood John's feelings. He's got a bitch of his own, apparently, and he would have done just the same. It'll be in his favour at the trial, even though it won't be mentioned. A nod is as good as a wink and all that.

'Once you've seen John, we'll let him out. He's feeling a bit

51

sorry for himself. He's a big lad, conscious of his own strength, and he doesn't like to think he let his temper run away with him.'

'Sounds like John,' I said. 'How's Biddy?'

'Could be worse. Andrew Thomas saw her this morning. She's in a bad way, but she'll pull through. He told me to tell you, by the way, that your splinting job wasn't at all bad – for a doctor.'

'That's the finest compliment I've ever been paid,' I said. And I meant it.

'Morning, Bob,' said John, sitting bolt upright on the bench in Cell 3 and trying to ease the pain in his ribs. 'Sorry you've got involved again.'

'I'd have thought you'd have had enough, John,' I said. 'Couldn't you just let the law take its course? That's what it's for.'

'I know,' said John. 'The law will see to those buggers for

stealing the fish. But it won't do much for Biddy. All I did was to redress the balance a bit; sort of thumping by proxy. The two clouts I gave that feller were for Biddy and her pups. I had time to give him three – one for me as well – but I turned the other cheek.

'Did I ever tell you I was a pacifist. . . ?'

CHAPTER 5

Peargate

The small town of Peargate lies on a corner between Sanford-on-Sea and Tadchester, hemmed in on two sides by the River Tad before the Tad goes out to the estuary to meet the River Trip and the sea.

Facing Peargate across the Tad lies the holiday village of Stowin. There had been talk for many years of a bridge to link these two places but the expense of such a project made it quite impracticable. While the Councils of both places interminably debated the possibilities of a bridge, Jones Bros capitalised on the lack of direct communication by running an hourly ferry across the river.

Peargate was a boatbuilding town. Boats had been built there since time immemorial. The boatyard had sometimes changed hands, craft had often varied in size, but boatbuilding continued there and probably always would.

The peak of activity was during the Second World War when landing craft were produced by the hundred. Although Peargate shipyards did produce some large ships, they specialised mainly in boats of tugboat size and smaller.

The main yards were in the town near the dock. Up the river, towards Tadchester, there were smaller, family boatbuilding yards that specialised in pleasure craft, rowing boats and small fishing boats. Tadchester, not to be outdone, had its own yard to the east of the town where sophisticated hydrofoils were built.

Peargate could claim more pubs to the square yard than any other part of the Somerset coast. Although a few of the terraced houses were being taken over as holiday homes, the vast majority of Peargate people were the product of many generations who had lived in the same houses. They were a close-knit community, excellent smugglers and fishermen.

Peargate architecture was unique: a maze of narrow streets, each with a low-level drain running down the centre. The houses were in long terraces with back-to-back yards. The streets themselves were so narrow that a car could only just get along one way, the sides of the car almost brushing the windows and house doors.

Main drainage had improved the sanitation problems and made the central street drains unnecessary. However, many a noisy reveller had the contents of a chamberpot thrown over him as he walked down the street, which not only quietened him but illustrated the previous function of the central drains.

In spite of the fact that Peargate was smaller than Tad-chester, there was tremendous rivalry between the two towns. Both had their own regatta, each advertised the event as the most important regatta in the west of England. Peargatians thought of Tadchester men as farmers and colliers. *They* were the only real sailors.

One sailor who sailed out of Peargate was Jonathan Blake. He was a captain and master mariner and responsible for the sea trials on all the new diesel tugs. He was a small, quiet man with a sharp, pointed beard, a completely bald head, and a weary look on his face as if he had all the world's troubles on his shoulders, which for most of the time I knew him, he usually had.

I met him soon after he arrived in Tadchester from Devon-port to take up his appointment with Peargate Shipbuilders. He had arrived with five children who he somehow managed to look after on his own. I was introduced to him when he bought the house belonging to Gladys, our senior receptionist. Gladys had shared the large house with her mother. After her mother died, she moved into a flat near the surgery.

I could never work out how Jonathan Blake coped. He saw me fairly regularly in the surgery for odd aches and pains, indigestion or insomnia, all minor ailments that masked the real problem: that the situation he had on his hands was more than he could manage.

His wife had deserted him. Before deserting him, she had caused him an awful lot of worry by being wantonly promiscuous. She was quite happy to leave him to bring up their five children, three girls and two boys, whose ages then ranged from the youngest boy of four to the eldest girl of fourteen. Somehow between them they managed to do the cooking, the washing and the ironing. There was little outside help available and it was doubtful if Jonathan could have afforded it if there had been.

The two boys wet the bed every night, which must have considerably increased the laundry bill, and the general state of the house was chaotic.

Jonathan Blake's duties at the shipyard meant that when there was some new type of engine or new type of tug, he would have to go off on sea trials. Then, when the boat was ready, he would have to deliver it to the new owner and break in the crew. This meant being away from home for anything between three and six weeks. While he was away, one of the neighbours would usually keep an eye on the children. They were an unruly lot and very easily got out of hand.

When the eldest daughter became pregnant at the age of fifteen, fortunately it was by a boy who had a reasonable job and who was prepared to marry her and set up home. It meant one child less for Jonathan, but it also meant that the female head of the household had gone, thus increasing the strain on his domestic responsibilities. He would come to my surgery almost blank with fatigue, only some inner force keeping him going.

Jonathan looked desperately for another mate, as much to help with his domestic duties as to share his bed. When he could get a night off, he would go to singles clubs and dances. He had one or two near misses and one or two narrow escapes until he began an intermittent affair with Sarah. Sarah was twenty-eight and had three children of her own. She was also undergoing psychiatric treatment. That was Jonathan's kind of luck.

He used to discuss his lady friends with me but it was some time before I actually met Sarah. There had been a lot of to-ing and fro-ing, but eventually Sarah was installed in his home, adding her three children to his four.

At first the domestic side of the household improved but, as Sarah was prone to nervous breakdowns, she had to be admitted periodically to hospital, leaving Jonathan with seven children on his hands. He appeared to be a born loser, a sucker for punishment. But he seemed to be able to stagger on from one disaster to the next.

When Jonathan was away, Sarah was in nominal charge of the household. Mark, the elder boy, resented her. He was growing up now and did not enjoy having six brothers and sisters as opposed to three. He was a restless boy and had all sorts of brushes and problems with school authorities and the police. Mark was about sixteen when Jonathan was away on a five-week trip delivering a boat to Denmark. He had been found breaking into the local sports club and the police were called. There were various other troubles, including his interfering with a young girl.

A phone call from Sarah brought me news of the crisis.

Her solution to any problem was to get psychiatric help. She considered that psychiatrists were her personal friends. If Mark had been stealing, then he must see a psychiatrist. Police calling at her home were likely only to aggravate her own nervous trouble.

I did manage to get a psychiatrist to do a domiciliary consultation on Mark and the household in general. It was only when I received his report that I appreciated fully the home situation. Sarah had thought the crisis would be helped if she took stepson Mark to bed with her and comforted him by making him her lover. She even thought that Jonathan would be pleased at how she had handled the situation.

Sarah brought Mark with her to see me at the surgery. I

could hardly recognise him. Apart from the fact that he had his best suit on, he looked tired, with bags under his eyes, and terribly bewildered. Sarah, on the other hand, was blooming, dressed up to the nines.

'Doctor,' she said, 'I have had a marvellous realisation. I have been talking to my father from his grave, and life is better than it has ever been, and I don't want it to stop. Mark has only to hold my hand and all my vibes go. I have second sight; I can read people's minds. Although I am twenty-eight, my mind is that of a woman of fifty, and my body has returned to that of a girl of sixteen.

'That is,' she concluded, 'apart from my stretch marks.'

For more than half an hour she stumbled on, attempting to tell me something, with no real idea of what she was trying to say. It was all disjointed and senseless. It was a reflection of the guilt she felt about taking Mark to bed and the worry that at some stage she would have to face the issue of his father coming home. They left the surgery with their problems unresolved.

The next night I was off duty and out at a Round Table meeting. Sarah telephoned, wanting to speak to me. Pam, used to patients by now, fended her off.

Half an hour later Sarah rang again, saying that she wasn't a patient but a personal friend of mine. Could I speak to her? Again, Pam told her I was not there.

I learnt the full story from Jack Hart the next day. He had been called by Sarah after she failed to contact me and he was left with little alternative but to get her into hospital. When she got there, having agreed to go in, she refused to be admitted. 'I have no money,' she said, 'otherwise I would quite happily go in as a voluntary patient.'

Jack Hart duly forked out £5, but when Sarah found that she could not take Mark into hospital to share her bed, she refused again.

Over the next few hours her condition gradually deteriorated. She thought she was God and had a divine message to pass, forgiving people for their sins. Eventually she had to be admitted to hospital under a compulsory order after an awful,

59

undignified struggle, with strait jackets and tranquillising injections.

Three days later Jonathan Blake and Mark came to see me at the surgery. Jonathan had managed to get himself flown back from Denmark. He had his usual worried frown.

'I'm still trying to sort this out, Doctor,' he said. 'It's all my fault. I'll just have to fix it that I don't go away again.'

My heart bled for him. In spite of the fact that his common-law wife had just been bedding down with his elder son, had made yet one further incursion into hospital for mental breakdown, with nothing to suggest that her mental instability would ever be any different, Jonathan was determined to have her home again in his chaotic household where each disaster was only a preparation for a bigger one.

Nobody could help them. We had offered every possible facility available under the National Health Service and various voluntary organisations. The whole situation was a tremendous education to me. How *did* people in Jonathan Blake's position somehow get up and keep on going? I wondered what eventually would become of the children. As they grew older and left home, would they re-create this same environment for themselves? Where did any of them find the incentive to go on living in this complete chaos?

But when I looked back I remembered times when Jonathan's family were as happy as sandboys, when the eldest daughter's baby was christened, when they were all planning to go on a camping holiday.

I talked to wise old Steve about it.

'You must remember, Bob,' he said, 'that all people are different and seek their own satisfactions in their own way. But,' he said with a smile, 'some are more different than others. I think you could put the Blakes in this category . . .'

*   *   *

Another patient who fitted well into Steve's 'different' category was Miss Monica Patterson, a spinster in her early fifties who lived in No. 5 Railway Cottages, close to Tadchester Station.

There were seven cottages in all and their description belied their elegant appearance. They were originally grace-and-favour houses built by the Great Western Railway for their more senior employees in south Somerset.

Although the GWR had disappeared with nationalisation, the residual families of the favoured employees were allowed to continue living there. Monica's elderly mother was the actual tenant of No. 5; Monica herself would be safe as a sitting tenant after her mother's death, as she worked in the local office of British Rail.

The health of old Mrs. Patterson merited regular fortnightly, or at least monthly, calls, and my visits to No. 5 were always traumatic. When Monica was at home, she kept up a constant tirade about her mother, saying what a cross she was to bear. Although she wished her no ill, she said, she hoped the Good Lord would take her quietly in her sleep.

When the old lady was on her own, she kept up a tirade about Monica: she never did anything round the house, she would never eat, she spent all her time smoking and drinking, and left her old mother to prepare the food, not only for themselves but also for the assortment of cats in the household.

It took me some time to realise that it was old Mrs. Patterson who was keeping the household together and doing most of the cooking and cleaning. Her eyesight was very poor and she had difficulty in getting about. She was, however, a lady of some dignity. When her husband was alive she had been able to travel all over Britain because of the special facilities offered by the railway to its employees. She was well informed, well read, well groomed, and just despaired of her daughter.

Monica was thin, round shouldered, sloppily dressed, with long, untidy hair, nicotine-stained lips and always had a cigarette, lit or unlit, hanging from the corner of her mouth.

I was always trying to encourage her to give up smoking and to eat a bit more. This usually brought a sharp retort: 'I'll stop smoking when you give your pipe up, and I'll start eating when I see you have lost a bit of weight. I wouldn't like to look like you.'

That, I thought, was a bit below the belt. Admittedly, Pam's cooking and the contentment of married life had filled out my former whippet-like outline, and my smelly old pipe might not have appealed to everybody, but I *was* the doctor, damn it.

It was an uphill struggle keeping old Mrs. Patterson going. She was coming up to ninety. I think the main reasons for her longevity were two driving ambitions – one was actually to reach the age of ninety, and the other to outlive (for some old and bitter family feud reasons) a sister-in-law.

'I want to see *her* off,' said Mrs. Patterson. 'I would also like to see the cats happily at rest before I go. I know Monica won't miss me.'

It was an unhappy household, with the daughter waiting for her mother to die to allow her to make some effort to shape her own life.

I had to admit Mrs. Patterson to hospital a couple of times but she somehow survived the worst bouts. When she was away, Monica almost stopped eating altogether and relied on nicotine and alcohol to keep her going.

On one of my routine visits to the house I was greeted by a beaming Mrs. Patterson.

'Guess what?' she said. 'My sister-in-law died yesterday.'

Forty-eight hours later I was called by Monica. She had found her mother dead in bed.

Mrs. Patterson had a look so serene that she had come as near to dying with a smile on her face as anyone I have ever seen. I wondered what had caused this bitter feud between her and her sister-in-law, but now I would never know.

Mrs. Patterson had achieved only one of her ambitions. She was still eleven days short of her ninetieth birthday.

I worried about what Monica would make of her life with her mother gone. Her dress and gait were so slovenly that I wondered how useful she was as an employee. Although there was no medical need to visit Monica, I used to pop in from time to time just to make sure that she was eating. My suspicions about her worth as an employee were confirmed six months after her mother died, when Monica was retired prematurely.

Without her mother and without the discipline of work, Monica steadily deteriorated in just about every way. She seemed to have no friends. Anybody who tried to help her got a very sharp rebuff. I would find her sitting in a chair, smoking, with a few bottles of drink by her side. When I tried to encourage her to take an interest in things outside the house she would respond sharply: 'I'll live my own life in my own way, Doctor, thank you very much. I just want to outlive the cats, then it's a handful of sleeping pills and I'm out of this world.'

Monica did less and less. Her sharp tongue gradually cut her off from almost all offers of help. Only one selfless neighbour struggled on to do things for her.

There were reports of Monica being found drunk in the street, but when I questioned her about her bruises, she said she had fallen down the stairs.

Twice she had to be admitted to hospital for attacks of pneumonia. She discharged herself as soon as she was on her feet. 'They wouldn't let me smoke in my oxygen tent,' was her chief complaint.

Relatives called and offered to take her back with them. She refused. She became even slacker both in her personal hygiene and her dress. Her clothes were stained and the general air of offensiveness was such that the pubs she used to visit, one by one, refused to serve her. It was exactly like the latter half of *The Rake's Progress* – a remorseless deterioration of body and mind.

She was continually falling. In one of her falls, she broke her hip. I had hoped a longer stay in hospital would give her time to pick up, but she came home looking more emaciated, hardly able to walk, having once more discharged herself against medical advice.

In a way, I was quite fond of her. She didn't make life easy for me, and had deteriorated into an awful, filthy mess. But she always enquired about my own health and that of the family, scolded me for working too hard and encouraged me to take things easier.

Though the hip had mended, there was some limitation of

her walking and she moved even less often. She would sit in her armchair, surrounded by bottles of booze, cigarettes and a few bars of chocolate, with a cat on her knee.

I found calls to Nature no longer roused her enough to leave her chair. I made the mistake one day of sitting on a chair she had recently vacated, to feel rising damp penetrating my own trousers after I had been sitting for a few minutes. It meant I had to go home, change, and send my trousers to be cleaned. This was an experience I had had before with much older patients: with Monica it was a horrifying sign of premature degeneration.

I arranged for the district nurse to come every day to attend to Monica. The one faithful neighbour still came in each day also, but I could not stop the decline. Most of the brass and assorted pottery that her mother had so proudly displayed round the house began to disappear as Monica sold them to keep up with the cost of her drinking and smoking. The electric fire was kept burning day and night, with the Electricity Board pressing for payment of bills which she made no attempt to settle.

She lingered on somehow, still bright enough to tell me off, but slowly and progressively getting weaker, until she lapsed into coma and was once more admitted to hospital.

It was after she had been admitted for what, in fact, turned out to be her last illness, I learnt the full story of Monica.

'She wasn't always like this, you know, Doctor,' said Mrs. Wilkinson, her neighbour. 'She used to be very smart. She was away on Government service during the war. When she came back to the railway, she had a friend here at work ... a very good looking woman. They used to have a right wild time of it. They were inseparable, always went everywhere together. They had planned to retire a bit early and share a home. Then one week her friend gave in her notice, left the district and went off to live with a lady solicitor.'

It was from then on, apparently, that Monica started to go downhill. She had never mentioned any of this to me, if indeed she had discussed it with anyone.

It all made sense now – the deterioration, lack of will to live, lack of interest. Monica had been suffering from a broken heart – broken by another woman.

Monica never regained consciousness and died three days after this last admission to hospital. But she still had one surprise in store.

Mrs. Wilkinson came to see me. 'There is a letter for you, Doctor, left by Monica in case she died.'

I opened the letter. It was the real old Monica again.

'Doctor Bob,' she wrote, 'You have got to do something for me. You know better than anyone else what a useless life I have led these last years. I want you to make certain that my body is left for medical science. Just make sure you get on with it. I can, perhaps, at last do something useful for somebody.'

Then followed strict instructions that there was to be no funeral.

There was a PS: 'Thank you for looking after me.'

I had never arranged for anyone's body to be used for medical science before; usually the deceased had arranged it beforehand.

I found it far from easy, I rang several of the teaching hospitals and they were not interested. If Monica had had some obscure condition, they would have been very interested, but the poor woman had just died of neglect.

I rang the anatomy professor at my own hospital and explained the position. He at first said no, then, when I said she had left this express message and he was my last hope, he replied 'Right ho.' I was able to leave it to him to see that her body was transferred to the anatomy dissection room, where students could learn from her poor, wasted form.

I was so pleased and relieved that I had at last been able to arrange this. Somewhere, I could sense Monica smiling. Once again, and for the last time, she had had her own way. Some young and hopeful medical student, setting out to become a doctor, would now have a sounder base from which to go on and do his clinical medicine. Thanks to Monica.

What better memorial could anyone have?

CHAPTER 6

Innocents Abroad

Pam's father, Gerry, had been a lost soul since the death of his wife. He found it extremely difficult to settle down without her. He came over to us and stayed frequently but refused to come and live with us permanently, saying that we had our own lives to lead and he did not want to interfere.

His delightful wife, Bill, had died of cancer just four days before our daughter Jane was born.

Gerry lived at Winchcombe, fifteen miles away, and drove back and forth along the estuary road to see us. He still played his violin with various orchestras but, as he had only moved down from Leatherhead to Winchcombe a few years before, he had few local friends and depended on us a great deal for his social life.

When we visited him we could see that the general care and upkeep of his house was beginning to deteriorate; it lacked a woman's touch and was really more than he could manage. After a great deal of thought he decided to advertise for a housekeeper. He put an advertisement in *The Lady* and one or two other magazines. It must have been one of the very few advertisements ever for a musical housekeeper. It read: 'Housekeeper wanted. Must be a proficient piano player.' Gerry wanted somebody to accompany him with his violin.

During the next few weeks he travelled all over the south-west of England interviewing potential housekeepers. He came back after one particular sortie saying, 'She was a fine woman ... lovely home ... cooked a marvellous meal ... but when I asked her to sit down at the piano, she banged out "Home, Sweet Home". I wouldn't have her touch my piano.' Gerry had a baby grand that was his pride and joy, although he never played it. It was destined for Pam when he no longer wanted it.

At last, Gerry found himself a housekeeper – Vera – a diminutive, rather quiet woman who came from South Wales. It was all fixed up without our help. And Vera was a good piano player! What we did not find out until later was that she was a hopeless cook and knew nothing about housekeeping.

Gerry had been quite happy about this and was fully aware of it. 'I'll do the cooking and cleaning,' he said, 'providing she plays the piano properly.' He had never suffered fools gladly, and we were very worried for Vera's sake because she had sold up house and home and her own piano to join him.

It worked marvellously for the first month. As far as I could gather, they played music virtually all day, with Gerry nipping off to prepare food between bars. After that we saw the relationship gradually deteriorate.

In all, the association lasted four months. We liked Vera. She was an unobtrusive, pleasant woman and I think she had an awful time.

We did not even hear that they had parted until Gerry came over one day and airily said, 'Oh, I gave her a week's notice a fortnight ago. I don't know where she has gone.'

'Why did you do it?' we asked, feeling concerned that Gerry was now back to square one.

'Well, listen to this,' he said.

He produced a tape recorder from his pocket, and on it was a recording of them both at practice.

The recording was awful. There was a strident, out-of-time violin playing discordant notes which were held together by virtue of finely balanced piano playing from someone with an immaculate touch.

Gerry was not nearly as good on the violin as he used to be. I think he entered another world as soon as he picked up his bow, and his faculties for criticising his own playing seemed to be the first thing he left behind.

'Well? What do you think of it?' asked Gerry.

'I have heard better,' I answered, guardedly.

'I should think so,' said Gerry. 'She was bloody awful. Just not up to my standard. She had to go.'

Poor Vera. We did not know where she had gone. Somewhere she would be trying to set up home again, and without her cherished piano that Gerry had made her sell before she joined him.

We racked our brains about how to cope with Gerry and looked at properties nearby so we could keep a closer eye on him. In the end it was Eric who made the suggestion.

'You have plenty of land down here by the river,' he said. 'Why don't you tack on a flat for your father-in-law?'

It meant knocking down one or two precious trees, but Gerry was all fired with the idea. After planning permission and the usual ups and downs of dealing with bureaucracy, we began to build a bungalow with a door into the side of our house. It had a kitchen, bathroom and bedroom, a separate garage for his car and a huge picture window in the lounge, overlooking the estuary.

The building work seemed to go on for ever. There was dirt and mud that daily found its way into the house. Gerry came over every day, breathing down the workmen's necks.

*   *   *

Finally it was done, and he moved in. By this time we were all in a state of complete exhaustion. We needed a holiday. Pam yearned for the sunshine. Jane was a bit too young to take abroad, but we knew that Zara, her godmother, would take care of her.

John Bowler offered to lend us a Volkswagen dormobile which would sleep four.

Our friends Peter and Jane Churchill offered us the use of a villa in Grasse for a week, and we planned a circuitous route down to the French Riviera, spending the middle of the holiday in the villa.

Gerry looked on wistfully as we made our arrangements.

'I've always wanted to go on a trip like that to France,' he said '. . . and I'd like to see Peter and Jane again. I'd pay my share of expenses.'

We had little alternative but to ask him to join us, so signed him on as ballast, philosopher and financial backer.

We had the Volkswagen for a few days before we left. John Bowler had assured us that it would cruise effortlessly down French motorways at more than sixty miles an hour and we could do five hundred miles a day without really trying.

At last the great day came for our departure, the boys jumping around with excitement – they had never been abroad before. It was a wrench leaving Jane with Zara, but we knew she would be well looked after. So we all climbed aboard and set off for Southampton.

The Volkswagen was so easy to drive. The driver was high above the road with a good view of all that was going on, and the passengers could sit comfortably round a table in the back – very similar to a dining compartment of a railway carriage.

Cards and other games could be played on the table and, with the stove at the back, a running buffet and refreshments could be served all the time.

There was a small luggage rack on the roof and, as usual, we travelled heavily. We piled up the rack with folding seats, cricket bats and tennis rackets, and a tent. The luggage rack was right over the driver's seat and, with the accumulated pile set on top, in distant silhouette we looked like a four-wheeled unicorn.

The sleeping space in the van was limited, hence the tent. The idea was that Pam and I would sleep in the body of the vehicle, with the table and everything collapsed to make a bed. This was Pam's particular bête noire: the more we collapsed things, the less room we seemed to have, and we ended up almost standing on our heads before we got some sort of order out of the blankets and mattresses, knowing that we would have to take them all up in the morning and repeat the procedure the next night.

The boys were to sleep on two stretchers under the canvas canopy which could be extended above the top of the Volkswagen. The stretchers were similar to railway luggage racks but narrower and more uncomfortable. Gerry was to sleep in the tent.

We crossed the Channel by night ferry and arrived at Le Havre at seven in the morning, with a whole day's driving ahead.

With a bad experience of a camping trip to Spain behind me, I had selected a superior, five-star-plus site near Vichy for our first night in France.

Vichy is only about 350 miles from Le Havre. Knowing the capabilities of the machine I was driving, I knew that the journey would pass like a flash. I had noticed in England how smoothly the vehicle went, and we had clocked a steady 35 miles an hour. I was now looking forward to letting it rip on the straight French roads.

I kept a gentle cruising speed until we were clear of Le Havre. Then, with an endless, straight, wide road ahead of me,

I plunged the accelerator into the floor and waited for the Volkswagen to take off.

Our speed rose steadily – 35, 36, 37, 38, 39, 40 miles an hour. The wind was whistling past the windows. Then a slight upward slope. With my foot still pressed down the speed registered 40, 39, 38, 37, 36, 35 – and this was the fastest the damn thing would go.

I looked forward to a full and frank exchange of views with John Bowler when I got back, but I realised that this was three weeks and many wearisome miles away.

To make our scheduled spot, we had to drive solidly all day, hardly daring to stop for refreshment, and eventually arrived in Vichy at about eight o'clock that night.

It was Easter, there was a bit of a nip in the air, and we looked round hungrily for this super camping site. There was a restaurant marked in the guide so we would not be cooking this evening. We followed the signs expectantly. As it grew darker the signs led us to a field containing one caravan.

I checked and rechecked. No mistake. This was the camping site with all the stars. The closed grey buildings at the far end of the field must have been the restaurant, showers and shop. I checked my guide once more and discovered what was wrong: the site did not open until June.

*   *   *

I was weary and saddlesore; the children were cold, hungry and fractious. Gerry, on his first camping holiday, at the age of seventy-five, was beginning to look a bit grey round the lips. I started to put up his tent whilst he sat shivering in the driving seat of the Volkswagen. I put up a camp bed in the tent and zipped two sleeping bags together on top. I undressed Gerry, who had now stiffened in his long johns, threaded him into the sleeping bag and pushed a hot water bottle in with him. I gave him a huge tot of whisky and zipped up the tent . . . wondering whether he would still be with us in the morning.

I stumbled back in pitch darkness to the Volkswagen to find

Pam in hysterics, trying to make a bed on the floor of the vehicle. On the front seat the boys were whimpering that they were cold, tired and hungry . . . and when could they go to bed? Please?

Eventually we got everybody sorted out, had a cup of coffee made from the rest of the water in the kettle that had been boiled for Gerry's hot water bottle, and settled down for the night.

I woke to a chilly morning, with a watery sun shining through the mist. The children were stirring. By lighting a little cooking stove in the van we soon created enough fug to make it warm enough to get dressed.

I had to face the question of whether Gerry was still alive. I walked to his tent to find it empty.

'Oh, God!' I thought. 'What next?'

In the distance I could see something bobbing up and down above the waist-high boards of the gentlemen's urinals so dear to the French. It was the top half of Gerry. Thank God. Presumably both halves were alive and functioning.

We put up a table outside for breakfast. Gerry, to whom food was very important, walked up and down, beating his arms on his chest, with a small dribble of saliva from one corner of his mouth in anticipation of the forthcoming bacon and eggs.

Gerry was one of those rare people who prefer to eat standing up. On this occasion he excelled himself, standing at a table in the middle of a French field with the spring sun shining on him, dressed in a peaked cloth cap, tweed overcoat, red and white spotted bow tie, yellow cardigan, and black leather gloves.

Nattily attired, he stood eating his bacon and eggs with relish. A passing Frenchman on a bike almost dropped off in astonishment. '*Ces Anglais!*' he muttered. Yes, we could still show them a thing or two . . .

After a wander round Vichy we packed up and headed for Avignon. The further we travelled south, the warmer it became, and we began to pass through vineyard country, with rows and rows of grape-covered hills – or what would be grape-covered hills, for at this time of year the vines were just short

brown sticks, like thousands of small soldiers standing in order, waiting to be reviewed.

For the first time since we had left Southampton I began to feel cheerful, but had my cheerfulness cut short by Gerry. I am no mechanic, but Gerry had once run a garage of his own. He sowed a seed of doubt in my mind about whether the foot brake was working properly. I was sure it was, but once having been unsettled I was testing the brake every few minutes and knew that I would be apprehensive until we had made our night stop. I also knew that Gerry would not settle until we had the whole thing re-checked by the Volkswagen agent – if there was one – in Avignon. Knowing Gerry, this could easily put us a day behind schedule.

I approached Avignon heartened by the sunshine but chilled with the thought that the next camp site was one star less than the miserable site at Vichy.

I checked in the guide. The site was supposed to be open all the year round, but I had begun to lose confidence in myself as a planner.

We found the place easily. It was spacious, the sun was still shining, there were trees and green grass, and all the things the Vichy site hadn't – a shop, showers, toilets, and a restaurant.

The blueness had started to leave Gerry's lips as we reached the warmer climate. He now had two dribbles of saliva, one in each corner of his mouth, brought on by the knowledge that we were going to dine at a French restaurant that night. To mark the improvement in our situation he deigned to take off his tweed overcoat, but firmly stuck to his cap, bow tie and leather gloves.

We chose a pleasant spot to pitch our tent, and parked the Volkswagen. There was hardly anyone in the camping site. We went up to the restaurant in the evening and had the full works: potage, moules marinière, rosbif and chips, a dessert and some delicious Camembert, all accompanied by a litre of wine and followed by coffee.

It was the first proper meal we had had for a couple of days. Trevor and Paul managed to make two mountains of chips disappear, diluted with several bottles of Coca-Cola. Gerry was able to bed himself down this night. He was improving.

Next morning Gerry and I shunted around Avignon for the Volkswagen agent. Eventually we found the garage, who thought the brakes were perfectly all right. Gerry, however, insisted that they should be bled and a whole day was wasted going through this unnecessary procedure. The frustrated workman who carried out the bleeding operation under Gerry's eagle eye must have thought he'd got a right couple of bleeders here.

In a happier frame of mind we set off the next day for the Mediterranean coast. I now accepted that we would be flashing through the countryside at 35 miles an hour and once I had reconciled myself to the idea, it made the driving that much easier. I still could not get Gerry to take his cap off.

We wanted to camp as near to the sea as possible and found the most delightful, tree-lined camping site in the beautiful little bay of Agay, halfway between St Raphael and Cannes.

We pitched our tent twenty yards from the water and parked

the Volkswagen next to it. Here we had everything – a restaurant, bar, clothes washing-machine, washing-up places, showers, and a shop, as well as the sun and the sea. It was even warm enough for Gerry to take off his cardigan and jacket, but he stubbornly stuck to his cap and gloves. The only time on the whole trip he had been without these two protectors was when we had our meal at the restaurant in Avignon. Even then I had to remind him to take them off before he sat down.

'This holiday's getting better all the time,' he said.

We had several days in this camping site, exploring the villages nearby and on day trips to St Tropez and St Raphael. The sea was cold but we all managed (except Gerry, of course) to have a swim. I think he felt that if he had gone into the water his cap and gloves would never have dried out.

We then packed up the tent and Volkswagen and travelled north-east to Le Rouret, a village near Grasse, where Peter and Jane Churchill were providing a villa for us.

The sun-bathed villa was picturesque: there were grapes on the outside walls, olive trees in the garden, and Gerry found he had an interior sprung mattress to sleep on.

'This is heaven,' he said.

It must have been, because he took off his cap, took off his gloves and settled in a deckchair in the sunshine with a bottle of wine by his feet and a handkerchief with a knot in each corner thrown over his head.

There were flowers to greet us in the villa, and we were completely spoilt by the Churchills. They showed us where to shop, bought us wine, and Peter had a day off work to take us all for a picnic.

Peter was one of the most delightful, spontaneous, warm men that I have ever met. He had an infectious gaiety about him; there always seemed to be a party wherever he was, and I can understand how willing people would have been to work for him during his heroic wartime exploits with the French Resistance. He was generous to a fault, kind and patient. He and his sweet wife Jane made a pair of perfect hosts.

Our picnic outing was a day to be remembered. Peter got up

early and went to Cannes market to buy trout for lunch. He was running an estate-agent's business at this time and actually had a bar in the boot of his car for entertaining customers. On lifting the lid of the boot you saw an array of bottles and glasses which would compete with most cocktail cabinets.

Peter was amused by the French sense of humour, or lack of it. He told me that one day in Cannes he was reprimanded by a gendarme for not having his parking disc. He apologised profusely to the gendarme, then said, 'How can I put this right? Have you ever had a rum and Coca-Cola?'

'No,' said the gendarme.

'Aha!' said Peter. 'It will be my pleasure to introduce you to it.'

So, in the middle of a busy Cannes street, he lifted the lid of his boot to open the bar and poured a good measure of rum and Coca-Cola. The gendarme loved it.

'Have another one,' said Peter.

'*Merci*,' said the gendarme.

So Peter poured another measure of rum and Coke, which

the gendarme began to drink with obvious enjoyment.

'Will you have a cigarette?' asked Peter.

'Good heavens, no,' said the gendarme, his manner changing as he came briskly to attention. 'I couldn't possibly smoke – I am on duty.'

Peter said the main point of the story is that whenever he tells it in France, nobody laughs or sees anything funny in it.

We all packed into Peter's large car to go up to the Gorge du Loupe for our picnic. A friend of Peter's from the Resistance days had the gravel rights to a canyon, and it was to be our private picnic place for the day. A stream threaded its way between the tall cliff sides of the canyon, joining together deep pools. The blinding sunlight was broken by patches of shade as the canyon ran its irregular course.

We jumped out of the car and ran to the edge of the canyon. Looking back, we saw Gerry still sitting in the car and waving, so we waved back and hurried on. We looked back again to see if Gerry was coming, and he was still waving. I thought it was strange, even for Gerry, for him to be sitting inside a car at a spot like this on a blazing hot day. On looking back once more I saw that the waves were becoming quite agitated.

We rushed back to find that Gerry had not been waving, he had been beckoning for help. As we had jumped out of the car the door had closed on his thumb, trapping it. If the door edges had not been lined with rubber piping, he could easily have lost his thumb. I wondered how he was going to get his glove on over his sore thumb on the journey home.

We had a marvellous day. Peter grilled his trout over charcoal by the side of the canyon. We had an unlimited supply of drink from Peter's bar, the sun shone, and the owner of the canyon, who was a marksman in the French Olympic rifle team, came to have a drink with us.

The boys had the time of their lives racing up and down cliffs, jumping into pools and throwing stones into the blue, crystal-clear waters of the gorge.

To try and repay, to some small extent, Jane's and Peter's hospitality, we took them out for a meal one night. An attraction at the restaurant was a tame rabbit which could drink with the best. The boys made a great fuss of it. The wine and conversation flowed. It got later and later, until we suddenly realised that two rosy-cheeked little boys in their red blazers were fast asleep in their seats.

We stayed as long as we could in our villa in Le Rouret, deciding to make the trip back to Le Havre with one night's stop only. We parked that night in the grounds of a château. As we had to make another long drive next day, we didn't put up the tent. Trevor slept on the front seat of the Volkswagen, Pam went up into one of the luggage racks, and I shared a bed with Gerry. It was an unforgettable experience – he actually kept his cap and gloves on in bed.

Pam says it was the most uncomfortable night she had ever had in her life. She had backache for weeks afterwards and now, many years later, still swears if she has backache that it started that night in the Volkswagen.

And so back home. Mission accomplished.

'What about next year?' said Gerry. 'Now I know what is involved, I will be able to get some proper gear.'

I wondered what that meant ... bowler hat, gauntlets, and cricket pads?

CHAPTER 7

Home Town

One of the drawbacks of Tadchester was that anyone with ambition had to leave. By virtue of the town's size and position, there were limits as to how far people could go in many careers. In such fields as engineering, planning, journalism or the arts, the ceiling was soon reached in Tadchester. Fortunately this did not apply to general practitioners: in fact we were particularly lucky in having access to our own hospital.

I attended many farewells of bright young Tadchesterians, leaving the warm comforts of mother Tadchester to venture abroad. Abroad meant anywhere more than fifty miles' distance of Tadchester: it could be Taunton, Salisbury, or even London, though some of course did go overseas.

At least two thirds of the ambitious young men who left Tadchester eventually returned. It wasn't because they had failed in whatever profession or work they had chosen, it was because they had never ever really settled outside the town.

Most often it meant coming back to jobs in Tadchester that carried less kudos, and certainly less money than they had when they were working away. It meant a reduced style of living, but none were looked on as failures. The very fact that they had returned to Tadchester confirmed in the eyes of all the local people what bright young men they were.

Those who returned all said the same thing: it was quite a good idea to go away and have a look round other places if only to realise that there was no place on earth better than Tadchester.

And there was much in what they said.

*   *   *

Tadchester was a friendly town, which enjoyed many amenities – the country, the river, pleasant houses – and was not too far away from some of the larger centres. Most important of all, Tadchester was a community, a familiar community where you knew most of the people who lived there.

It was the comfort of belonging that brought people back, and belonging and mattering is perhaps more important than anything.

I welcomed back many of these bright young men. Sometimes they brought a wife from outside Tadchester, bringing fresh stock to the community. Most of them had taken a Tadchester wife with them before they left giving a double incentive for their return.

One person whom I was not pleased to see returning to Tadchester was Marjorie Charteris.

Before her marriage, Marjorie, daughter of Commander and Mrs. de Wyrebock, was one of a trio of ladies who had made my life uncomfortable in Tadchester. Her ambition at the time was to be Mrs. Clifford . . . and it was only because of constant vigilance and evasive action on my part that she didn't achieve it.

Poor Marjorie had the disadvantage of having one of the largest sets of prominent teeth that I have ever seen. Her passion was horses (which she closely resembled), and before her marriage she had run one of the Tadchester riding schools. She had become engaged to her husband Paul Charteris about the same time Pam and I had become engaged. I think Pam was as relieved as I was.

Marjorie and Paul had moved away some time after her

80

parents' deaths and I was surprised when she came back, alone, to Tadchester. Later I gathered that she was divorced. She bought her old riding school back and with her two small daughters went to live in a house in its grounds. Her two children, poor things, had inherited their mother's rows of prominent teeth.

Marjorie was very formal about her return and sent us cards letting us know she was back. Pam said we would have to ask her round for a meal. I hated the thought. Marjorie took a bit of shaking off once she had set her cap at you, and now here she was again, fancy-free and presumably looking for somebody to help share her riding school.

We had a little dinner party for her with Kevin and Janice, Zara and Eric, and the enigmatic Mr. Nin. For some reason, possibly the smell of horses that seemed to follow Marjorie wherever she went, our Cairn terrier Susie just would not leave her alone. We eventually had to shut Susie in the kitchen.

I felt something furry squeeze past my legs. Susie! She must have sneaked back into the room when Pam had brought in the food. I put my hand down under the table to see if I could find her.

As I felt around, a delighted smile appeared over Marjorie's face. Susie was nosing the inside of her thigh.

Kevin noticed my groping around, and Marjorie's smile, and almost exploded with laughter into his soup. I dragged Susie out, but for the rest of the evening Marjorie kept smirking at me. The rest of our guests could hardly restrain themselves from giggling. Even Mr. Nin looked far from inscrutable.

I was worried that, after what appeared to be an attempted indecent assault by me, Marjorie might launch into Operation Wedding Bells again, Pam or no Pam. But I was saved by a small dark stranger.

Two months after she had moved in, Marjorie was joined by a diminutive and weatherbeaten jockey, who had apparently been the cause of the divorce. They made an incongruous-looking couple: the large toothy Marjorie and her tiny bandy-legged partner. It was difficult to see what they had in common

but perhaps he hoped one day to ride her in the Grand National.

*   *   *

Tadchester had had a hospital of some sort for at least as long as written records had been kept. The present hospital was a compact, two-storey building erected in 1938.

This hospital was the town's pride and joy. It had been financed by the town, and built by the town, and its running costs were carried by the town.

Before it was built, the doctors and surgeons somehow managed to work from St. Mary's Maternity Home. It must have been hard work, making do with no lifts, narrow staircases and a very primitive operating theatre.

Before the National Health Service, people paid for their hospital treatment if they could afford it. If they had no money, there were sponsored beds and special funds to see that no one lacked medical care.

The doctors attending gave their services to the hospital for nothing (having honorary appointments) apart from three private rooms out of the seventy beds available, where they treated their private patients.

Steve Maxwell and Henry Johnson remembered these days well.

'My god, we knew what work was in those days, Bob lad,' roared Henry. 'There were no weekends off then, just two weeks' holiday a year.'

Apparently the most time anybody could take off each week was a half day, and then only when things were slack. There were surgeries both Saturday morning and Saturday evening, and early Sunday morning the doctors did a round of the hospital before spending the rest of the morning doing the week's major operating list.

The senior partner of the group before the war was a Dr. Tubb, the first man in Tadchester to have a car. He was apparently a giant of a man with a huge head, and was referred to affectionately by his patients as 'Old Golliwog'. He was in practice in Tadchester for nearly fifty years, and lived well; in those days doctors were very important members of the community, with large houses and servants.

He, like Henry Johnson, had been Mayor of Tadchester, and was still well remembered by the older patients of the town.

Dr. Johnson used to work under Dr. Tubb. He learnt a lot from him, they said. (I couldn't imagine Henry working under anyone. I would have loved to have seen it.)

We were very fortunate to have the hospital facilities. It allowed us to be real doctors, taking overall care of our patients and treating them both in and out of hospital. Henry Johnson was an excellent surgeon, good enough to know when surgical conditions would be better treated in more specialised centres such as Winchcombe, Bristol or London. Many of his contemporary GP surgeons would have a go at anything, regardless of the result. Henry Johnson could cope with all emergencies, but he knew his limitations. He reckoned that if you had to have something like your stomach out, you were better having it done by someone who did this operation about a hundred times a year, as opposed to his once or twice in an emergency.

The coming of the National Health Service caused some changes in the running of the hospital. Every patient had free treatment and free medicine, which was welcomed. The doctors who had previously worked for nothing were paid for their services. Although some found this rather *infra dig*, on the whole it was welcomed. The administrative staff, which had consisted of two hard-pressed secretaries before nationalisation, increased to four. It had risen to fifteen when I joined the practice and has been steadily rising since.

A great boon was that expensive new equipment could be obtained on demand, and the hospital no longer had to go round cap in hand. But strangely, it was this last benefit that the town reacted to most. Many of the functions held by the town were to raise money for the hospital. The Carnival held during the summer when the town was full of holidaymakers was the year's big money maker. Now, without a major fund-raising incentive in the community, the town lost some of its direction. It was as if the hospital had been taken out of the townspeople's hands. The x-ray machine that they had struggled and skimped and saved for now belonged to someone else.

The Carnivals went on each year, but never quite on the same scale, or with quite the same enthusiasm. There were many other worthy causes to donate to, but it was not the same as keeping your own hospital alive.

Tadchesterians had always looked after their own, and found it difficult to accept that someone was taking over their responsibilities. There would be a gap in their lives until they found something else to worry about and expend their energy on.

It was very much like a family looking after a dying relative at home. While the loved one was still alive, they didn't really have to make decisions: every waking moment was devoted to taking care of the patient.

Often it would appear, especially in the case of a very old and mentally confused relative who had taken a lot of looking after over a long period, that loss would be a relief to the family, that the bereavement would let them get up and get on with their business.

In fact this was seldom so. The loss of an elderly relative who had been looked after for a long time, too often left a void, a lack of direction. The relatives who had been doing the nursing never quite got going again. They had lost their corporate discipline, and sometimes this led to the break-up of even close-knit families.

*　　　*　　　*

Henry Johnson *was* Tadchester Hospital. He was on every committee, had a finger in every pie, and ran the whole concern as a benevolent dictator, National Health Service or no National Health Service. No hospital or group secretary could ever tell Henry what to do.

But there was a wind of change blowing. More consultants were being appointed at Winchcombe and appearing at Tadchester to do sessions in the specialities. As GP hospital consultants retired, they were being replaced by full-time consultants. It suited me: for about twelve years I had given anaesthetics at Tadchester Hospital – always conscious of the fact that I had not been trained in this speciality – and was crushed when I lost a child during an operation. I welcomed the appointment of a full-time anaesthetist which enabled me to retire from anaesthetics altogether. But Henry was concerned with the wider issues.

'We have a fight on our hands lad,' he said. 'One day they will be wanting to shut this place down.'

'Rubbish, Henry,' I replied. 'They couldn't do without the casualty services we give – especially in the summer – apart from all the other care that's available here.'

Henry's predictions began to come true. It was insidious at first. A new maternity hospital was built at Winchcombe and St. Mary's Maternity Home was shut down.

Everybody welcomed that, both doctors and patients. St. Mary's had no proper facilities and was in a poor state of repair. Once I even had a dog come into the labour ward and lift its leg against a table when I was just delivering a baby. The whole situation was very unhygienic but strangely, and I don't know why, we never had a cross-infection amongst the babies.

The patients looked forward to having their babies in this brand new Winchcombe hospital, with specialist care to hand. We doctors, although we were loath to admit it, looked forward to being called out of our beds less often, and were pleased to have the responsibilities of difficult confinements taken off us.

Unfortunately the first mothers to go to Winchcombe were delivered by a doctor who could not speak English, and obviously was not as gentle with women as the Tadchester doctors. And in Winchcombe's sterile surroundings there would be outbreaks of cross-infections between babies that had never occurred in the very unsterile surroundings of St. Mary's.

The Tadchester GPs found they had lost a precious area of communication without their young mothers and babies; they were also losing some of their skills, as the number of babies we delivered became fewer and fewer.

Though it was clearly progress to have babies born in the best surroundings in the best and most specialised hands, it took several years for both doctors and patients to adjust to the new regimes.

I bemoaned the situation to Steve one day.

'Yes, Bob, I know how you feel,' he said. 'But like everything else, if you don't keep moving forward you tend to move backwards. And remember, nothing is ever always pure gain. If you gain something, then you are bound to lose something else. It may not be much, but in the widest terms, there is no such thing as pure profit.'

The next news was of a five-year plan. A large new hospital was to be built at Winchcombe and all the small hospitals in the surrounding twenty miles would be phased out or used for some other purpose. This was national policy. All hospitals were going to be big hospitals. It was the only economic and efficient way to run a proper health service, said the planners; small personal hospitals were expensive to run and inefficient.

Tadchester Hospital was to be run down, and eventually turned into a home for the chronic elderly sick, covering a much wider catchment area than Tadchester and its surroundings.

There was tremendous uproar locally, protest meetings and a Save Our Hospital fund. Henry especially was furious. 'Nobody's going to touch my hospital while I'm alive,' he said.

I asked Steve's opinion again. 'Change is bound to come, Bob,' he said. 'We must keep on exploring. I think in time this over-centralisation will prove to be a mistake – but it's got to be tried.'

'What about Tadchester Hospital?' I asked.

'I reserve judgment on that,' Steve said with a twinkle in his eye. 'I've yet to see anybody get the better of Henry.'

One by one, all the small hospitals began to be shut down. Tadchester, ruled by the fiery Henry, held out in its normal function until his retirement, when it was turned into a geriatric unit.

Many years later, when practically every small hospital had been shut down, one of the powers-that-be, some nameless and faceless person – probably an accountant – had a brilliant idea.

With the high cost of keeping patients in the large hospitals, it would be a good idea if small hospitals were opened in some small communities. Patients who did not need major medical or surgical treatment could be looked after by their own general practitioners, by nurses from their own communities, and close to their homes so their families would not have problems in visiting them.

I thought this was absolutely marvellous: as soon as they had managed to shut all the small hospitals they were starting to open them again. One step forward, one step backwards . . . or was it the other way round?

One evening I sat down and wrote a letter to the Ministry of Health:

'Dear Minister,' I wrote, 'I have an excellent suggestion for a building that would make an ideal community hospital for the town of Tadchester . . .'

CHAPTER 8

Life and Death

Fay Thurton died suddenly and unexpectedly one night. Pam and I were out to dinner and came back to find a note that Jack Hart had pushed through the door, breaking the sad news.

Fay Thurton was a plump, bustling little woman, aged sixty-seven, and had gone to work the morning of the day she died. Her life was centred round the care of her husband, Ernest. Ernest was ten years older and one of those patients with chronic chest disease who somehow keep struggling on, year after year, with hardly any physical reserves. There were recurring battles during many nights to revive him with varieties of intravenous injections that miraculously brought him back from the almost dead. If anybody at any time had asked me about his life expectancy, I would have said it was two or three months – and I would have said the same thing over a period of six or seven years.

I had come to know the Thurtons quite well as they were almost neighbours of ours. Our new riverside house, although still in the town of Tadchester, enjoyed a village-type atmosphere, the fifty or so houses around us making up a community. And Fay and Ernest were two of its members.

The two had married when Fay was in her late twenties and

Ernest was in his late thirties. Before her marriage, Fay had worked behind the bar in the Star pub on the road between Tadchester and Sanford-on-Sea. After her marriage she worked every morning cleaning at a boys' boarding school at Sanford-on-Sea and, as well, did the cleaning of St. Mark's Church, the small church that served our small community.

In her busy life Fay still found time to bake all her own bread. Whilst I fancied myself as a breadmaker and would from time to time make a batch of wholemeal loaves, if I ever swapped one of my loaves for one of Fay's I would find out what real breadmaking was all about. The first windfalls from our apple trees went to Fay in return for pounds and pounds of her stewed-apple preserve.

Ernest was one of the nicest types. In the time I knew him, he was well enough in his better phases to keep his allotment going. He had a greenhouse by the back door of their cottage in which he could potter around even on days when his breathing was especially difficult.

When I called round after receiving the news of Fay's death, I found poor Ernest completely bemused. He was the one who had been battling with death for so many years; it was unbelievable that his plump, vigorous little wife, so cheerfully involved with life, should be the first to go.

'She went to work this morning, Doctor,' he said. 'I told her she worked too hard ... she didn't have a sit down until this afternoon, then tonight, when I went upstairs, she was sitting up in bed, reading. Normally she always put my pyjamas out, but today she hadn't. I said "Where are my pyjamas?"'

'She turned to me,' said Ernest, 'and gave a little gasp, and then she was gone. She had been a bit giddy over these past couple of weeks, other than that she had been perfectly well.'

Ernest had a neighbour – Samuel Bell – with him. They had worked together when they were younger. Ernest, with his life shattered in one brief moment, did not want to go to bed, so we three sat up talking. I knew he had spent most of his working life making cricket bats. It was only that night I heard the full story.

'I left school when I was twelve, Doctor. It was during the First World War, when you were allowed to leave school at twelve if you were going to work on the land. When I was thirteen, I got a job with Burroughs, the people who make cricket bats, and I worked for them fulltime until I was sixty-eight, then I went part-time. I think I had just stopped when you first arrived here.

'I used to travel all over England at one time finding willow trees, choosing them, felling them, and bringing them back to be split up for cricket bats. I was very lucky, Doctor; I always had a job, and they looked after me. I had a gold watch when I had been with the firm fifty years, and several international cricketers still used to come and see me after I had retired.

'You were lucky to have work between the wars,' he said. 'If you got a job, you hung on to it. Many of the youngsters were out of work. For those that were in, it was often three days' work a week for married men, two days' work for single.'

I suggested that he came back and spent the night with us. I did not want him left on his own.

'Not to worry, Doctor,' he said. 'Thank you for asking me, but I don't think I'll go to bed tonight. Samuel will sit with me for a while.'

'Yes,' said Samuel, 'Don't you worry, I'll keep an eye on him.'

I called daily for the next few days. Ernest's brother and sister came down from Yorkshire to help with the funeral arrangements. Ernest's health was generally so poor he wasn't able to do a great deal himself. I let him have some tablets to help him sleep, and something to take on the day of the funeral.

Pam and I went to the funeral. There were fifty or sixty villagers there, mostly the older ones. This had been a great shock for all of them as Fay was almost a generation younger than most of Ernest's contemporaries.

The Reverend Wood gave a simple service. He said we would remember Fay for her cheerfulness and busyness around the community, her work as a cleaner in the church, her help with the mobile library. At first it seemed sad that there was no more to say about her. On the other hand, the simplicity and fullness of her life couldn't really be recorded.

I feared for her husband now that she was dead. After all, she had kept him alive, kept him going. He stood erect behind the coffin, breathless as he walked, following it to the graveside. I made sure that I was close to him as we left the churchyard. I had the feeling he could so easily collapse, but he did not. I even had to tell him to walk more slowly.

It was arranged that he would go up to Yorkshire to live with his brother and sister. The funeral was on a Thursday; he was going the following Wednesday. His cottage was owned by the Burroughs Cricket Bat Company so there was no property to sell. He was just going to clear up his possessions and go.

In a way I hoped that he might have died in those intervening few days. Without Fay I was sure he would find it difficult to manage.

But he did not die, and he did go away. I feared for him in strange surroundings in spite of the fact that his brother and sister were going to look after him. There was no alternative; he needed both a nurse and a housekeeper.

One of the local farmer's wives said to Pam as we walked back from the church, 'Isn't it awful? Fay died on Saturday, Ernest is leaving on Wednesday. They have lived practically the whole of their lives round here. In no time at all we shall probably forget both of them.'

I knew I wouldn't.

*   *   *

I found, in general practice, that I depended very much on my senior partners for dealing with problems that went beyond normal medicine and prescribing. So much of medicine has to be learnt after you qualify, and so much of medicine (in fact the major part of medicine in general practice) is the sheer management of people. As the old boy I met in a pub over celebration drinks the day I qualified said, 'So you are a doctor now. Don't forget a doctor's main job is to buck us all up.'

I remembered a time when I was a Bevin Boy at Dinnington Colliery in Yorkshire when we had a new colliery manager. He was straight from university, with an honours degree in mining engineering. He said the first day at his new job his first problem was to deal with two women who had been caught stealing coal from the pit tip. What was he to do with them? They had not included it in his honours degree curriculum.

Similarly, in medical school they did not tell us how to manage a situation where a wife had been beaten up by her husband, where the main causes of ill health were poor housing, poor income or just total unhappiness.

There was no instruction on how to cope with the bereaved. This was a major problem. Although I had the refreshment of delivering on average three babies a fortnight, I had at the same time to cope with three bereavements. It was never possible to forecast how much any particular bereavement would take in terms of my time, patience and energy.

I began to learn some things about people. I found that the people who had been the most happily married often coped better with the death of a partner than did those who had been unhappily married. In marriages that had not been going too well the sudden death of a partner sometimes resulted in the remaining partner reacting violently out of sheer guilt.

Reactions included attacks on doctors and nursing staff with wild allegations of negligence and malpractice. It had to be somebody's fault; there must be somebody to blame, be it the doctor, the employer, the seller of a faulty car, or one of a host of other 'suspects'. There would be a true and heart-rending exhibition of grief about the loss of the love of their life.

It was strange how the effects of bereavement manifested themselves sometimes. Couples who had a complete and happy life in the fullest physical terms, with full physical communication between each other, although they grieved tremendously after losing a partner, usually managed reasonably well. The bereaved who seemed to suffer the most and grieve the most were often those couples where there had been a lack of physical communication even to the point of an almost nonphysical relationship. I had imagined that it would be the physically compatible who would be the ones who had the most trouble in coping, but it was this other group, in my experience, which was more bereft. Perhaps their lack of physical expression was channelled into a higher form of spiritual communication. Whatever it was, this group of people seemed to suffer the most.

It is impossible to generalise. It is unlikely that definitive papers could ever be written about these circumstances. But the longer I stayed in practice, the more aware I became of what was likely to happen in particular circumstances.

In the general management of people's health, so often we treat the symptoms and not the disease. The disease perhaps may be an unhappy home life, unhappy marriage, unhappy work, unhappy day-to-day living situation – all emerging as some sort of medical condition, either real or imaginary, psychiatric or organic.

I wondered sometimes how much impact we really made on the course of people's lives and health, or whether we were just doing a temporary repair job ... putting a patch on a leaking psyche, which would blow again before very long.

*   *   *

After ten years in practice I had already seen various groups of drugs go through complete cycles. A drug would start by being the new wonder drug, to be followed by other similar wonder drugs. Their imperfections would become apparent with use. They would be dropped, and then perhaps they would be picked up again because their benefits outweighed their disadvantages. Then there would be some new look at their new situation. It would be decided that a particular therapy, prescribed for many years, was completely ineffective against the condition it was meant to cure and that, in some cases, the symptoms and side effects it created were worse than the original condition. It is quite likely that some of the treatments that we have seen over several decades for, say, high blood pressure, will be found not only to have been useless but actually harmful.

The difficulty in assessing any medical treatment is that you cannot measure the result of a particular doctor giving a particular preparation to a particular patient. Two doctors giving the same preparation to the same patient might have completely different results. It is impossible to measure the effect a doctor has on a patient, particularly one he communicates with. In a way the further we go forward, the further we go back, and we go back realising the imperfections of the things we prescribe. We realise that we have to treat people not conditions, that we must begin to treat people as a whole, and the whole includes their background, their family, their objectives, their aims and ambitions.

They were dangerous times when, because of my accumulating experience, I began to think that I knew about people. I was confident that I could predict how events would take place, how a particular situation would run. The patient, often influenced by my positiveness, would further believe in me and help implement any course I suggested. It was usually just when I thought I had begun to know something as an irrefutable fact that I would be brought down to earth with a bump. And so it was when the Suttons arrived to live in Tadchester...

*   *   *

I had been in practice about ten years when I had to look after the Suttons' seven-year-old son. They had recently moved to a large house on the Dratchet Road, two miles outside Tadchester. Their son was ill when they arrived and, from the letters which accompanied his medical records, I saw that he had been seen by the very best people in the country. His medical condition, as far as was known, was incurable. It was a type of degeneration of the nerve fibres in the body.

When I first saw little Charles Sutton he was confined to his room. He crawled about a bit on the floor, talked quite chirpily and was the very-much-loved only son of middle-aged parents.

I used my first couple of visits to get to know him. I knew of no specific treatment that could help him at all. After my second visit, his parents took me on one side and asked, with tears in their eyes, if there was any doctor, anywhere, they could ask for another opinion. They had heard there was a good children's doctor in Taunton – would I make an appointment for him?

I was as kind as I could be to them and said I was happy to make arrangements for him to see anybody they liked, but I thought there was very little that could be done.

As I thought, the child specialist in Taunton gave the same answer as all the other specialists. Nothing could be done, and the child had about six months to live. Charles was seen by specialists from Bath, Bristol, Cardiff, all giving the same answer: there was no hope for this boy.

When I was next called out to Charles, the parents requested that Stephen Maxwell came. I felt badly; you cannot be all things to all men but when patients change to other doctors, for whatever reason, you feel slighted. I had done a tremendous amount for the Suttons and thought we were on the best of terms.

Steve was non-committal about it. 'I am quite happy to see this boy, Bob lad. Apparently they heard somewhere that I had won a paediatric prize when I was a student and they would like my opinion of the situation.'

I saw no more of the Suttons and heard little from Steve about them until, six months later, I saw Charles's death announced in the local paper. This coincided with the arrival at the surgery of a most beautiful silver tea service for Steve, from the Suttons, with a note thanking him for all he had done.

I was extremely puzzled. I had done all that I could. I had sought every opinion that I could, and all of them were the same. As far as I knew, Steve Maxwell had sought no further opinion, and the child had died exactly as everybody had predicted.

I popped into Steve's room at the end of evening surgery. He was sitting at his desk like a wise old owl, smiling at me over the top of his gold, half-rimmed spectacles.

'Come in, Bob, and sit down,' he said. 'What can I do for you?'

'Tell me, Steve,' I replied, 'about the Suttons. I obviously made a big boob somewhere. Where did I go wrong, and what did you do when you got there?'

Steve said, 'I looked through the piles of notes about this poor little lad and through all the reports of the dozen or so specialists he had seen. Then, when I saw the child and the parents asked me what I thought, I said I thought he had every chance of getting over it.'

'Yes,' I said, 'but he didn't get over it. There was no chance of him getting over it. And yet they are obviously very grateful for all you did.'

'Yes,' said Steve, 'they have rather overdone it in terms of the gift. But as they explained to me after little Charles died, they knew all along that there was no chance of him recovering. But they wanted somebody to come to them and give them hope so that the last six months of his life would be a positive struggle – with the prospect of him getting better all the time – rather than six months of sitting down just waiting for him to die. It meant for the parents that the last six months of little Charles's life were lived with some kind of hope and had most of the strain taken from them.'

I realised as I left Steve's room how much I still had to learn about general practice . . . and people in particular.

CHAPTER 9

Down on the Farm

The first Christmas following the death of Pam's mother had been naturally a quiet one. The Christmas after that, when time had helped to abate the grief, was to be just the opposite. Pam's mother, Bill, a great lover of life, would not have had it otherwise.

The jollifications were enhanced by the presence of Ron Dickinson, our junior partner. For two years previously he had spent Christmas with his parents up North, but now he decided to sample the Tadchester festivities.

It was a tradition at the hospital Yuletide party for the doctors to be dressed up by the nurses in outrageous fancy dress costumes. This year, I was to be a Dalek, and was stuffed, protesting, into some sort of outsize dustbin. Even that, though, was preferable to my first year's costume. Then as Batman, I had to dress in a cloak and a pair of sheer – and embarrassingly revealing – black tights. The tights didn't keep out the winter winds, either.

Poor Jane, at that time still a few weeks off her second birthday, was terrified by the whole proceedings at the party and screamed inconsolably when she saw me getting out of my giant tin can. Pam had to take her home, missing the rest of the

junketing and my carving of the turkey on the children's ward.

Paul and Trevor, however, whose appetites could politely be termed healthy – and impolitely gluttonous – loved every minute of it. They spent the whole time happily being stuffed with pop, sweets and biscuits by nurses and patients alike.

Ron Dickinson was dressed up by the casualty nurses as a kangaroo, and it was exactly right for him. He bounced round the hospital to the squeals of the nursing staff and kept on bouncing until New Year's Day. Every party he attended he seemed to finish up in his underpants and covered in beer – the perpetual student.

He was nicknamed Peter Pan by Henry Johnson, and very aptly: in all the many years I eventually knew Ron, he never seemed to age.

Our Tadchester Christmases were very much centred round the hospitals, and each hospital tried to outdo its rival. Ron bounced round each one, was the life and soul of every party and, as he was still a bachelor, made many of the young nurses' hearts flutter.

One New Year's Day, however, he met his Waterloo. Tadchester Rugby Club had chosen this day to have their annual dinner. 'To sort of round off Christmas' was the reason they gave. I was fortunate in being on duty and unable to attend.

The unconscious Ron was carried to my house by four almost equally drunken companions at three in the morning.

They were a sorry sight, shirt-sleeved, clothes soaked through, on a bitter night with no idea of the whereabouts of their jackets, coats, ties – and in one case trousers.

I bedded them down on the lounge floor with a vomit bowl apiece. I turned on the electric fire and levered Ron onto his side, so that if he were sick there would be no danger of his choking.

As I turned him, he stirred. One eye opened.

'Happy New Year boss,' he said. 'Just bacon, eggs and kippers for breakfast, please . . .'

* * *

After the excesses of Christmas and Hogmanay, the first few weeks of the New Year can hardly be anything but an anti-climax. Body, brain and bank balance need time to recover.

John Denton introduced me to a delightful way of easing into the New Year and reminded me that in the midst of what felt like death, we were indeed in life.

'Morning, young Bob! How's your head?' boomed the voice over the phone, in an accent from darkest Manchester. (John had opted for the country life after his army service, but had been born and raised in the industrial north.)

'It's still attached to my body, John,' I said. 'But otherwise it's hard to say.'

'I've got something that should clear it,' said John. 'We start stripping trout tomorrow morning at the fish farm, and it's always a bit of a social event. Plenty of fresh air in the barn and a hair or two of the dog that bit you.

'As it's Saturday tomorrow, I thought you might be free to come over. Bring Pam and the kids, too: they'll enjoy it.'

'Sounds fun, John. What time?'

'About ten. Should have a decent crowd in by then. Oh, and bring a bottle.'

'What kind?' (My muddled brain was trying to connect a bottle with stripping trout of their eggs: I thought perhaps John might be presenting me with some roe.)

'Any kind you like,' said John. 'So long as there's summat in it.'

'Ah. A bottle as in bottle party?'

'By 'eck, lad. You catch on quick. See yer.'

I arrived at the fish farm *en famille* and *avec bouteille*, to find a handwritten sign which read STRIP SHOW THIS WAY, followed by an arrow pointing to a large barn. Inside the barn was a sight neither I nor the family will ever forget.

In the middle of the floorspace stood four large galvanised tanks, filled with water and pulsating with fish, two such tanks on either side of a long bench. Standing on each end of the bench were a couple of smaller tanks and, in the middle, a clutter of large bowls and dishes. Over this, as if it were an altar, John supervised his helpers in the ritual of stripping the fish.

The bench was lit by an electric bulb dangling from the ceiling. What was really amazing was the rest of the barn. It was lit by the warm glow of candles, dozens of them, burning on trestle tables, benches, boxes and tea chests.

Standing around, or sitting on an assortment of stools and chairs – in one case a plush leather armchair – were dozens of people. They were of every age and station, from the youngest ragamuffin of the town to several magistrates and well-to-do members of the county set. Even scruffy old Charlie Sloper, veteran cadger, was there, wandering around the tables and helping himself to other people's food.

Everybody had brought something to eat and drink, from humble cheese sandwiches and cider to smoked salmon and champagne. A portable record player in the corner played the Vaughan Williams *Fantasia on a Theme* by Thomas Tallis. It was as if we had walked into a wooden-walled cathedral where some holy rite was being enacted.

'You could say,' said John, as he stripped away at the trout,

first squeezing out the eggs from several hen fish into a bowl, then the milt from a couple of cock fish, 'that this is life, this is. The beginning of life for several million creatures. All happening before your eyes. There's not much that's holier.'

'You old fraud,' I said. 'Going around all year pretending to be a no-nonsense, down-to-earth, practical unbeliever – and now turning into some kind of high priest.'

'Just the other side of the coin,' said John. 'Look at these fish. No creature is more practical, down-to-earth, no-nonsense than a trout. Just an appetite with fins. But they're performing a miracle here, with a little help from their friends.

'And look at them.' He gestured at the assembly, which was growing in numbers by the minute. 'They know they're witnessing a miracle. That's what they've come to see. That's why they're making an occasion of it. And by doing so they're creating the atmosphere that a miracle deserves.'

They were. It was an atmosphere such as might have existed in a medieval church, used as the real focal point for the village and the surrounding countryside, when religion was part of

102

daily life, and not just a burst of once-a-week piety.

'May I help, John?' I asked, wanting to get down to some practicalities before I was carried away on a wave of mystic euphoria.

'Aye,' said John. 'You've got the fingers for it. I daren't let some of these cack-handed buggers anywhere near the fish for fear they'd do some damage.'

Basically, trout-stripping is artificial insemination. To avoid hit-and-miss natural spawning, with its risks of under-fertilisation, of breeding from inferior or unhealthy stock, and of the eggs and fry being eaten by the adult fish – perhaps even the parents – trout farmers take control of the whole breeding process.

First of all, only big and healthy fish of good pedigree are used as 'broodies'. When a hen fish is lifted and her belly sags, swollen with eggs, then she is ready for stripping.

Stripping is simply stroking the belly with a wet thumb and forefinger, towards the vent, squeezing out the eggs into a clean dish. No force is used, and no attempt made to take eggs which do not flow easily, for fear of damage to the fish.

Three or more hens are stripped into the pan. Then a cock fish is stripped, to cover the eggs with milt, or sperm. On John's farm, often two cock fish are stripped into the same dish, in case one should be infertile.

The eggs and the milt are then mixed together gently by hand, covered with water, and left for about a quarter of an hour or until the eggs separate from each other. The eggs are now fertile. They are washed to remove dirt and surplus milt and, as 'green' eggs, are laid down for hatching or sold to other breeders.

Each fish may be stripped two or three times over a period of perhaps a fortnight, and then put back in the stock pond to recover and become 'clean' again.

As I stripped the fish, gaining confidence with each one, I could appreciate John's feelings about the creation of so much life: hundreds of thousands of new lives beginning every quarter of an hour. And I realised why the barn was so crowded and so charged with that indefinable atmosphere.

I was stripping merrily away, enjoying it more and more, when John said, 'Hey up, our Bob. You'll be doing me out of a job in a minute. Would you mind if this young gentleman took over?'

I turned to see a tow-headed, grubby boy of about twelve standing there.

'Hello,' I said. 'It's Tommy Thompson, isn't it?'

'Right,' said John. 'He's taken time off from pinching my trout to see where it all starts, haven't you, Tommy? Right, lad, get stuck in. But gently, mind . . .'

I was out with John on his beat once when he surprised Tommy Thompson in the act of catching trout with a hazel-twig rod and six feet of line. 'The best little poacher for miles' was how John described him, acknowledging an honourable adversary.

Whenever John came across Tommy in the act of poaching, the rules were that John made a lot of noise and Tommy vanished into thin air. Tommy knew the rules and observed them. For his part he never took more than a brace of trout at a time, and treated the river with respect.

Tommy was one of the many local poachers who were of great help to John in reporting the arrival of professional fish-thieves from outside the district, or of outbreaks of disease among John's beloved trout. 'The local villains earn their corn,' said John. 'There's hardly a spot of fungus on my fish that I don't know about within the hour.'

The ceremonial stripping went on to the accompaniment of eating, drinking, quiet conversation and subdued music. The big barn, normally cold and draughty, had warmed fuggily to the heat of the candles and the assembled bodies. The only jarring note in the proceedings came when John discovered Charlie Sloper pocketing (repeat, pocketing – Charlie never was fussy about dress) a large handful of fertilised trout eggs.

He was swiftly and unceremoniously ejected, cursing loudly and protesting innocence at the same time.

'What's the matter, John?' I asked. 'Did Charlie fancy some caviare for his tea?'

'Caviare be buggered,' said John. 'The little tyke was going to use it as bait. It's illegal for a start and deadly for a second. That short-arsed heap of rubbish can do enough damage to my fish stocks, without any free bait from me.'

When Charlie's curses had died away, I suddenly realised that for an hour or so I'd forgotten all about Pam and the children. I needn't have worried: they were so engrossed in everything that they'd forgotten all about me. Even Jane, who was only two, was entranced by it all.

For Trevor, Paul and Jane, that scene has remained one of childhood's beautiful memories. It came in useful to me, too, when it was time to tell each of them the facts of life. I didn't have to waffle on about birds and bees. I said simply, 'Do you remember the time we went down to the trout farm . . . ?'

CHAPTER 10

Love Me,
Love My Goat

Animals played a big part in the life of Tadchester and its hinterland. The houses I visited on my rounds were usually within sight or spitting distance of some livestock or other. Not surprisingly, animals were responsible directly or indirectly for a larger proportion of cases than a normal surgery was used to coping with.

My surgeries held too many surprises to allow for complacency, and whenever I lowered my guard, something got through and jolted me.

*   *   *

One of my firmest jolts was given by the Hamlins. The Hamlins were sort of semi-gypsies and divided their time between collecting scrap iron and sheep-farming.

There were about twenty-four in the whole family. Swarthy, dark-looking characters, they were friendly, good natured and well integrated into the town. They lived very much as a clan and their twenty-four included at least two lots of grandparents and various family groupings that were not always easy to determine. There were about fourteen or fifteen young children, but who belonged to whom I was never sure.

I confidently diagnosed impetigo when one of the Hamlin children was brought to see me with a weeping sore on his face. It was only when I had seen the fourth and fifth Hamlin child with this type of impetigo that I began to suspect I had made a wrong diagnosis. The children had sores on their faces, lips and hands. They did not seem to respond to my usual ointments. I thought I had better visit them at home.

Their homestead consisted of a group of disused Nissen huts turned into bungalows, standing next to a huge scrapyard filled with old cars, bits of railway line and all sorts of other metal objects. The heap of scrap seemed steadily to grow in size without anything ever happening to it, but it obviously provided the Hamlins with plenty of money: their run-down Nissen huts were cosily and lavishly furnished inside with clean curtaining, ornaments and pictures, very much in the gypsy tradition. There were also new cars, washing machines and TV sets, which could not have been provided for by the rather mangy flock of sheep they kept.

The flock of sheep were a legacy from the last war, when they were the Hamlins' answer to meat rationing. It was a simple philosophy – if you couldn't buy meat in the shops, then you grew your own, and if there was a bit left over you could always get a good price for it.

I found, in all, that eleven of the twenty-four in the family had these infectious-looking sores. Although I had seen similar conditions before, I had never seen anything quite like this.

I paid my respects to the oldest Hamlin – Gregor Hamlin, a wizened old man in his eighties, with a gold earring in one ear. He was not easy to communicate with. He had had a slight stroke a few years back which made speech difficult and he rambled on in a confused, disjointed way. I tried to talk to him about this epidemic amongst his family but all I could get from him was a shaking of the head and 'They got orf. They got orf'.

What they had got off from, I had no idea. I assumed it was some prison sentence from one of their less scrupulous deals. But this was no help to me in treating this unpleasant skin condition that was affecting so many of them.

Eventually I had to put all those contaminated on antibiotic tablets and creams. I agreed to go and visit them again as the numbers infected had now risen to fourteen and they could really justify a surgery on their home ground.

On a sunny evening when I made my next visit they were all outside clustered round Gregor as he talked to Andrew Faber, the vet, who was holding a limp-looking lamb in his arms. As I got near, I saw that most of my patients were very much better, even from a distance the infected areas of skin were hardly visible. As I approached Gregor he nodded excitedly at me, waving his stick.

'They got orf. They got orf!' he shouted.

I wondered again from what crime his family had been reprieved. It must have been something pretty stupendous to take priority over the skin rashes.

'He's right,' said Andrew Faber, holding up the lamb. 'I'm going to engage him as my assistant.'

By now I was completely confused.

Over a cup of tea in Gregor Hamlin's Nissen hut, Andrew patiently explained it all.

The sick lamb and most of the Hamlins were suffering from the same disease. It is primarily a condition of sheep but if bitten by or in close contact with sheep, human beings can pick it up. Its name is ORF!

Happily the treatment I had prescribed was the treatment that it required anyway, and it was one more deposit in my knowledge bank.

I got up to go. Gregor Hamlin looked up: 'You going orf now, Doctor?'

I looked down at my hands; they were spotless.

'No,' I said. 'Not if I can help it.'

*　　　*　　　*

Mark Adler was one of several freelance illustrator artists in Tadchester. In his anarchic appearance and attitude to life, he strongly resembled Spike Milligan – and some of the things

which happened to him were straight out of a 'Goon Show' script.

A passionate conservationist, he was one of the first to recognise the danger to toads from the road leading to a new housing estate. The road had been built over what was once a farm track, and passed a pond to which the toads migrated to breed every spring.

The migration route lay across the farm track, and for untold centuries the toads had faced no greater hazard than the occasional cart. But the road changed all that: suddenly they were being crushed in their hundreds beneath the wheels of fast cars and lorries.

The phrase 'Help a Toad Across the Road' had not yet been coined as a campaign slogan, but that was exactly what Mark was doing and it was from his lips that I first heard it. Several times a day, armed with a bucket lined with damp moss, he would patrol the road and gather up the toads which were making their laborious way across.

A motorist brought Mark to the surgery and left only after solemn assurances from Mark that he would be all right. Mark limped into the consulting room, the flattened toe of his right boot beginning to rise again from the swelling of the foot underneath.

I cut the boot and sock away to reveal a badly swollen and bruised foot with at least two bones broken.

'How do you like that, Doc?' said Mark. 'I went to help a toad across the road – and got run over.'

Apparently in his enthusiasm he had leapt out to snatch a toad from the path of an oncoming car. He got the toad all right, but as he turned to leap back, the car went over his foot.

'It was the driver who brought me here,' said Mark. 'Nice bloke, but not into the toad thing. He spent half his time fretting in case he'd done me some permanent damage and the other half calling me a bloody fool. Mind you, he was good enough to tip my bucket of toads into the pond before giving me a lift in.'

The experience gave Mark a respect – I was going to say 'healthy respect' but it didn't quite work out like that – for traffic on the road.

A few weeks later he was in again, the plaster cast still on his foot, this time with a couple of broken ribs and badly pulled muscles in one arm.

'After getting that big flat foot,' he said, 'I became paranoid about crossing the road. I looked right, left and right again, and wouldn't set foot on to the road until there were absolutely no cars, lorries, buses in sight.'

'Good thinking,' I said. 'So what brought this on?'

'I looked right, left, and right again ... not a four-wheeled vehicle in sight ... So I stepped out into the road ... and got run down by a horse.'

That was typical of Mark's enthusiasm, or perhaps obsession would be a better word. When he got a bee in his bonnet he would concentrate on it to the exclusion of everything else. This time he had been looking for motorised traffic in the middle distance, and the galloping horse from the local riding school, which must have been almost upon him, hadn't even entered his consciousness.

* * *

The riding school provided me with a steady flow of patients, mostly inexperienced youngsters who after a few lessons had become over-confident and taken a tumble, but Jim Fraser was the only parent I had to treat.

Jim, the son-in-law of the lovely old Mick and Alice, appeared at my front door one Sunday morning, supported by his wife, Philomena. There was no Sunday surgery, of course, and strictly speaking he should have gone to casualty at Tadchester General Hospital. But I was a friend of the family, and this did seem to be rather a delicate matter.

Jim stood there, knock-kneed, watery-eyed, and clutching the source of the pain which was roughly, or precisely, in the area of his masculinity.

'Sorry, Doctor,' said Jim. 'It's my ... phwarh ...'

He broke off, gasping and speechless. So Phil told me the tale as I helped Jim on his painful way indoors.

She and Jim had called at the riding school to collect their two children from their morning lesson. The pupils were still out on a cross-country canter, so the two parents walked across the back field towards the gate where the horses would enter on their return.

As they walked across the field, Jim saw a tethered horse whose rope had become wound tightly several times round its leg. The horse's head was pulled down by the rope and the animal was obviously in danger of struggling and hurting itself.

'I'd better sort this out,' said Jim.

'Are you sure you know what you're doing?' asked Phil. Jim was not exactly built like John Wayne and his love of horses far exceeded his experience.

'No problem,' said Jim. 'You just show 'em who's boss.'

With encouraging words of 'Whoah, boy' 'Steady, lad' etc. Jim tried to unwind the rope. The horse stood still, not that it

111

was able to move anyway, and Jim decided there was nothing for it but to pull up the tethering stake and unwind the rope from the free end.

Soon the rope was untangled and the horse was able to lift its head. Jim patted it professionally on the neck.

'Told you,' he said. 'All you've got to do is show 'em who's . . .'

At that very moment the returning horses and riders appeared at the bottom of the steeply sloping field. Jim's horse whinnied in recognition, reared, and shot off like a bullet.

Jim hung on to the rope and was towed at top speed down the field, leaping through the air in giant strides and landing each time with a jolt on the tussocky grass.

'He looked like the first moonwalker on earth,' said Phil. 'Apart from the screams it was very impressive.'

When the horse reached its old mates it stopped suddenly. Jim, who was in mid-bound, crashed sickeningly into its hind-quarters and collapsed spark-out on the grass . . . still clutching the rope.

'I say, who's that?' demanded the haughty-looking riding mistress.

'It's my *father*,' said young Laura, in a tone of disgust. 'He's being silly again.'

Phil went to the aid of the stricken Jim and busily patted his face to bring him round.

'Is he all right?' asked their son Richard. 'Only I've not had my pocket-money yet.'

Jim opened his eyes.

'All you've got to do,' he groaned, 'is show 'em who's boss . . .'

Examination of Jim showed some pulled muscles in his arms, shoulders and inner thighs, the last were the ones which were causing the pain. But apart from that there was no real harm done.

'I don't like to ask this,' said Phil, blushing. 'But has he done himself any mischief? I mean, will it have any permanent . . .? Will it affect his . . .?'

I cut Phil short to spare her embarrassment.

'Don't worry, Phil,' I said. 'It's very painful at the moment. But I can assure you that Jim will definitely play the violin again...'

*   *   *

Dogs figured in a number of cases; two in particular come to mind, along with the Tadchester Arms and the annual fair.

The fair brought lots of trade to the town, and the local pubs would hire casual bar-staff for the week it was on. It also brought lots of pocket-picking, petty pilfering and break-ins.

During one fair the Tadchester Arms was broken into. A locked and full till had been carried out bodily, the subsequent loss representing a big part of the profits of fair week. The following year the landlord, Geoff Emsworth, bought a surprise for would-be intruders in the shape of a trained, but very vicious, alsatian guard dog.

The night before the fair, Geoff hired a young student to work in the saloon bar.

'Start tomorrow lunchtime,' he said. 'See you here at eleven o'clock.'

Geoff was outside, dealing with draymen, when the student arrived.

'Just in time, son,' he said. 'Go behind the bar and through the flap into the cellar, and lift out the crates of light ale to make some space at the bottom of the steps. I'll see you down there.'

The boy went into the pub. Within seconds there were sounds of savage barking and screams of pain.

'My God!' said Geoff. 'I forgot!'

He ran into the pub, charged behind the bar and dragged the dog off the student, whose jacket had been ripped to shreds and whose arms were a bloody mess.

Geoff rushed him round to surgery. I stitched the boy up and gave him an anti-tetanus injection. He certainly was in a mess: it took thirteen stitches to repair the damage to his arms.

Geoff was beside himself with remorse.

'How could I be so stupid?' he said. 'I forgot he hadn't been introduced.'

That sounded crazy, but it was all that was needed to make the dog accept a stranger. It had been trained to accept people introduced by its owner, but to make life very unpleasant for anyone else.

The student was a brave lad. He reported for duty at the pub that same evening and was properly introduced. By the end of the night he was scratching the dog behind the ears – and the thing was looking at him with something very much like soppy love in its eyes.

I heard some strange reasons for unexpected pregnancies during my time at Tadchester. The heaviest crop – both of unexpected pregnancies and strange reasons – regularly came to light a month or two after the fair. There were always girls silly enough to believe the stories of sudden but undying devotion spun by the wandering fairground lads. And there were always girls mercenary enough to bestow their favours for a few free rides on the dodgems or a couple of illicit trophies from the coconut shies.

They would usually turn up at the surgery convinced that they were afflicted by anything but pregnancy. On hearing the news, their reaction was almost always the same: they just couldn't understand how it had happened.

However, one girl – Julie – understood exactly how it had happened.

'That damned dog!' she said.

'Pardon?'

This was one of the moments when my guard was down and a jolt came through.

'That dog and his cold nose!'

'I think you'd better explain, Julie,' I said. 'Either I'm a bit dim this morning or you've made medical history.'

Julie explained. She had met this lad who took the tickets for the Big Wheel. Name of Carlo (unlikely, but more romantic-sounding than his probable real name of Charlie). Carlo had dark wavy hair and ever such white teeth and had a way of looking at you which made you go funny all over. (I managed to stifle a yawn at this bit.) Carlo had said he could not do without Julie and that next time the fair came near Tadchester he would bring her something special, such as an engagement ring.

On the strength of this, Julie went with him after the fair had closed one night to the barn behind the Tadchester Arms, which Geoff allowed the fair people to use to store spares and odds and ends.

Among Carlo's odds and ends was a single bed mattress, and it was on this that they plighted their troth.

At a crucial moment during their plighting, when it was dependent on Carlo's restraint to prevent it being fruitful, the cold nose of a wandering dog alighting upon Carlo's naked posterior meant he lost his concentration and resulted in Julie's visit to the surgery.

Julie was unlucky all right, but Carlo would never know how lucky he was — that the damned dog wasn't the flaming alsatian...

*   *   *

One of the saddest animal tragedies I witnessed was not a goring by a bull, or a savaging by some huge dog, but the conflict between two schoolteachers and their pets.

Miss Geraldine Smith and Miss Marigold Bendle first came to Tadchester on holiday when they were student teachers at a training college in London. They fell in love with the place, and each year always managed to have two or three weeks together in the town.

After qualifying, Miss Bendle took a teaching post up in Cumbria, and Miss Smith stayed on in London on a post-graduate course, but their correspondence and the Tadchester holidays kept them in touch.

Miss Bendle finally finished up as head of the English Department at a girls' school in Chester, and Miss Smith finally made a headship at a small girls' school in Kent.

I once read a book on planning retirement. The author advocated that you should start looking for a place to retire in your early forties, buy a cottage there if possible, and over the years slowly build yourself into the community.

The author would have loved the Misses Bendle and Smith: they started planning their retirement at the age of nineteen.

Miss Bendle was a short, plump, good-natured lady, with long dark curly hair. Miss Smith was tall, slim with short cropped hair and an abrupt manner. In her mid-forties she took to wearing steel-rimmed spectacles, which increased her rather severe aspect. She was the sort of person you would imagine to be for capital punishment, against promiscuity and who would stand up whenever she heard the national anthem.

Over the years the two women became well-known and well-liked figures in the Tadchester area. Neither ever showed any desire to be married, and they were rarely seen in male company.

In their early fifties, actually on Miss Smith's fifty-first birthday, they bought their dream house: an end-of-terrace cottage overlooking the harbour at Peargate.

From now on, all of their holiday time was spent in Tadchester, pottering about and tinkering with their cottage, preparing for the time when they could eventually pack up work, and live together happily in retirement.

The time got closer and closer, until there was just one summer term before they could come and live in Tadchester for ever.

During this term, the pupils of both teachers must have suffered. Miss Smith and Miss Bendle were almost already living together in the house of their dreams. They wrote every day, full of excited plans and each hinting to the other that she was planning a surprise that would make their future days together even richer.

Miss Bendle's surprise was a big fluffy Persian cat, intended to give softness and warmth to their new home. Miss Smith's surprise was a strong and energetic bull terrier which they

116

could take for walks along the cliffs and watch chasing rabbits across the common.

I was called to the house about two hours after they had got together at their new cottage.

Miss Bendle's school broke up a day before Miss Smith's and she had arrived with her precious fluffy Persian cat twenty-four hours before Miss Smith.

I reckoned that I was called about an hour after two vets had been called independently. When I arrived one vet was stitching back some fur on a very nasty and bloody-looking area of the cat. The other vet was dealing with some very nasty scratches around the eyes of the bull terrier.

The two women, whom I am sure had not spoken a cross word in years, were screaming abuse at each other and at each other's pets.

I had to put five stitches and an anti-tetanus injection in Miss Smith's arm where her dog had bitten her when she tried to pull him off the cat.

I had to swab Miss Bendle almost all over with antiseptic as well as give her a shot of anti-tetanus: her cat's claws had ripped into her as it sought shelter from the attacking dog.

It was the end of the relationship. Miss Bendle moved out that night, stayed overnight at a guest house, then moved north to look after an old aunt in York.

Miss Smith stayed on at the cottage on her own for two or three months, and most afternoons could be seen walking her dog on the cliff. The dog was kept on a very tight lead, as if he was the last living thing in the world. Miss Smith was giving him no chance to get away.

Suddenly one morning, she too was gone. A 'For Sale' notice went up on the cottage and Miss Smith was never seen or heard of again.

*   *   *

The story of Miss Smith and Miss Bendle became almost overnight folklore in Tadchester. I was talking to Bob Barker about it one day.

'Definitely a case of love me, love my dog,' said Bob. 'But did you ever hear of love me, love my goat?'

'No,' I said, 'but I'm sure you'll tell me.'

'Some years ago,' said Bob, 'a church deacon bought the malthouse on the edge of the River Tad. Although it had river frontage it went quite cheaply: there was almost a sheer drop of sixty feet from the house to the river's edge. You could manage to get down the bank to the river side with a struggle, but what you could not do was keep the undergrowth in any sort of order. It had plenty of water and grew profusely.

'The deacon had spent some years of his ministry in Africa, and had observed the habits of the indigenous goats, that would eat anything and strip foliage to soil level. So he bought some goats. In no time at all his bank was cleared of foliage and he had the bonus of free goats' milk.

'The one snag to the whole scheme was the goats' affection for the deacon's wife. They followed her everywhere, and she was the only person they would allow to lay a hand on them, particularly at milking time. There was almost always one of the goats in milk all the time and needing to be milked every day. The deacon and his wife were never able to get away on holiday as a couple, or even have a full day out.

'The crisis came when the wife was taken ill. After only one day the goats' painful bleating could be heard clear across the river.

'Several people tried to relieve their feelings, without success. Then there was an imperious demand from the sick-room. The gardener led two of the goats upstairs, and the deacon's wife milked them from her bed.

'The deacon wisely said nothing, but after two days of having goats milked in his bedroom, he set off on a mysterious mission to the town. The next morning the goats had gone – 'stolen'.

'The deacon made a great show of getting in touch with the police, but the culprit was never found.

'However, for a few weeks one of the Tadchester butchers had goat's meat for sale, and Charlie Sloper had a rare spell of

affluence. 'A right toff, that deacon,' he was heard to say.

The deacon's wife, though grieving for the goats, did recover from her illness, and she and her husband lived happily ever after, or as happily as any couple could after such an experience.'

'Is that a true story?' I asked Bob.

'Yes,' said Bob. 'Quite true. I was a young church organist at the time, always willing to help – and I acted as link-man between the deacon and Charlie Sloper. And goat's meat isn't at all bad once you get used to it . . .'

CHAPTER 11

Deserving Cases

The National Health Service, comprehensive as it is, can never fully take the place of each looking after his own.

Two of my favourite patients were Mick and Alice, married fifty years and ... (the usual phrase here is 'never a cross word', but I've yet to come across a marriage of even fifty days to which that applies).

'A bloody good row at least twice a week,' was how Mick described their formula for married bliss. 'Clears the air something lovely.'

Mick was retired now, and his breathing and eyesight were such that he had had to give up his part-time job as lollipop man outside the local school. Alice worked on full-time in the Tadchester Hospital canteen.

It was Mick's health I had always watched, but it was Alice who suddenly fell very ill. They were an independent old pair, and by the time I was called Alice's condition had degenerated into pneumonia.

'How is she, Doctor?'

Little Mick stood blinking moistly, his hands still working through some rosary beads. (Mick and Alice were staunch Roman Catholics and much-loved members of St. Malachy's

Church. Only a few months before, a special mass had been said for their Golden Wedding and a surprise slap-up reception laid on by the congregation.)

'I didn't want to bother you at first,' said Mick. 'Alice was dead against calling you out, and she's always been so fit. But I knew she was badly when she stopped arguing. I know we're getting on a bit, but I can't lose her, Doctor, I can't.'

'She *is* poorly, Mick,' I said. 'But I've put her on antibiotics and she should improve within a few days. Now I want you to give her one of these tablets every four hours and two of *these* tablets every six hours. And make sure you . . .'

I broke off. Mick wasn't listening. Behind the tears, his eyes were filled with pain and fear. Fifty years is a long time.

'Tell you what, Mick,' I said. 'You'll have enough to do with the housework and things.' (I knew full well that Mick was in no state even for that.) 'I'll call on your daughter Phil on my way back and ask her to keep an eye on Alice.'

'No, no, Doctor. You can't do that,' said Mick. 'They're off up north tonight for a few days with their cousins up there. They've not had a break for a long time and their kids are really looking forward to it.'

'All right, Mick,' I said. 'Don't worry. I'll fix something.'

I fixed it very quickly. Mick needed looking after almost as much as Alice. Capable as the district nurse was, this was a job for family.

Mick and Alice had brought up seven children. Six of them were those of Alice's sister, who had died not long after her husband. Their own child was Phil – Philomena – now married to Jim. Together, Phil and Jim ran a little hairdressing business down in the town. Mick was right: they worked hard and needed the break. But this was a matter of priorities.

I called in at the salon, where Phil was taking the rollers out of a customer's hair.

'Right,' she said, after I had explained. 'Thanks, Doctor. Leave it to me. Jim, Mum's poorly. Could you finish off Mrs. Wainwright while I get things organised?'

Phil picked up the phone and rang the relatives up north, postponing the visit. Then she rang those of her 'sisters' who were on the phone and living close enough to be of help. That done, off she sped in her car, leaving Jim to attend to the remaining customers and to look after their two children that evening.

Within a couple of hours, Alice had been made more comfortable, Mick had been fed, the accumulation of pots in the sink had been washed, and the house had been tidied.

For the next week, Phil and the sisters kept up a rota of calls all through the days and into the nights. Phil had issued each sister with a list of the times and types of Alice's medicaments. Each got in whatever shopping was necessary, made a hot meal for Mick and prepared whatever nourishment Alice was able to take.

Then Alice started to mend. Phil called one morning to find her mother lying uncomfortably between two armchairs in the living room; Mick had been sleeping in these chairs to allow Alice to rest undisturbed.

'What the heck are *you* doing here?' demanded Phil. 'You're supposed to be upstairs in bed. And where's Dad?'

'Oh, poor lad,' said Alice. 'I could hear him in the night, tossing and turning on these chairs. With his bad back he wasn't getting a minute's peace. I was feeling better, so I came

122

down and made him swap. He's upstairs now, getting some decent sleep.'

Two days later, Phil knew her mother was over the worst. She called in on her way to work. Alice and Mick – Alice in her nightgown – were in the kitchen, arguing hammer and tongs.

'What's the matter?' asked Phil.

'What's the matter?' said Alice. Then, pointing an accusing finger at Mick, 'He's the matter!'

Mick shuffled uncomfortably, trying to look defiant and innocent at the same time. A difficult feat.

Apparently Alice had woken up feeling much better, and hungry for the first time since the illness. Mick had tottered upstairs, and was delighted to find her sitting up.

'Don't worry, love,' he said. 'I'm going to look after you. How do you fancy poached eggs on toast and a cup of tea?'

'I'd love some,' said Alice. 'But don't burn the toast.'

'Have no fear,' said Mick. 'I know just how you like it.' (He did: very lightly browned. But every time he had made toast in their fifty years together he had burned it to a cinder.)

Mick went downstairs and Alice sat on the edge of the bed expectantly. Twenty minutes passed, half an hour, forty minutes . . . Alice was beginning to feel chilled. And there was still no tea and toast. Not even a smell of burning.

Finally she went downstairs into the kitchen. At the kitchen table sat Mick, supping from a pint mug of steaming tea, and reading the sports section of the morning paper.

'Where's mine?' demanded Alice.

'Where's what?' said Mick. Then, as it all came back to him, 'Oh, 'eck . . . I forgot.'

I realised when I heard the story how right I had been to overrule Mick and call in Phil. I realised also that Alice was back to her old fighting self – thanks to a bloody good row – and that the long and loving marriage was safe for some years yet.

*   *   *

Nowhere in the dictionaries of saints or heroes does the name of

Mick Mitchell appear. This is some small attempt to rectify the omission.

I was making my last call on Alice, now fully recovered, just to make sure that there was nothing else I need do for her.

'How's Mick coping now?' I asked.

'Same as usual,' she said. 'Always under my feet. But I'll tell you something, Doctor: that little feller downstairs is a saint and a hero.'

I must admit it hadn't occurred to me to endow him with these qualities, fond as I was of the old lad. And certainly his recent performance hadn't been over impressive.

'I'll tell you about him,' said Alice. 'We'd arranged to be married, all those years ago. The banns had been called, date set, church booked and everything. It wasn't to be a posh do: times were bad and Mick was out of work, but we were going ahead with it.

'I was one of eleven kids. My dad was dead and my mother was having a real struggle to make ends meet. She'd got behind with the rent and the landlord was threatening to throw the whole family into the street.

'So Mick went and pawned his best suit, his best boots and his watch and chain, and paid the money to the landlord. That left him with no decent clothes to be married in, and with no job he had no hope of getting them back in time for the wedding. So he postponed it: he wasn't going to show me up by standing at the altar with patches on his pants. It was another six months before we got wed.

'Later on, my eldest sister, a widow, died and left six kids. All my other brothers and sisters had more children than they could cope with, so we took them in. For years Mick worked all hours God sent to bring them up, and somehow we managed it. Thank God for his best suit: it was in and out of pawn like a yo-yo.'

I said goodbye to Mick in the kitchen.

Shuffling nervously, obviously trying to remember if there was something else he'd forgotten to do for Alice, he didn't look at all saintly or heroic. But I knew better, and against Mick's

124

five-foot-and-a-bit I felt quite small.

There's another name I'd like to add to the list of saints and heroes (or heroines) – Alice.

Mick had taken on enormous burdens for her sake, but she had made sure he didn't carry them alone. And in these later years, with her love and attention – not to mention the bloody good rows – she never failed to let him know how much he was appreciated.

Thank God, I thought, that out of everything in this world they'd found what they both most loved, cherished and deserved. Each other.

$$*\qquad*\qquad*$$

A couple who could not, in the widest terms, be said to deserve each other were Major Hawkins and Charlie Sloper. They had been described as one of the funniest double acts since Laurel and Hardy.

Major Hawkins was tall, erect, brisk and immaculately groomed, the epitome of an officer and a gentleman. Charlie Sloper was the exact opposite: the local poacher and ne'er-do-well, pint-sized, dirty and unbelievably smelly.

As a lieutenant, Major Hawkins had been Charlie's platoon officer in France in World War One, and he used to say that for that alone he deserved a medal. Charlie was hardly an exemplary soldier: in fact he was the most scruffy, idle, scrounging, malingering excuse for a soldier in the whole of the Somerset Regiment.

Major Hawkins would groan every time Charlie's unshaven and grimy face appeared among the morning's defaulters. After listening to Charlie's wild excuses he would pass the appropriate sentence and mutter under his breath, 'Desert, you squalid little man. For God's sake, *desert!*'

But one day, during an attack on the German lines, Hawkins was blown badly wounded into a flooded shell hole. He owed his life to Charlie, who leapt in after him and kept his head above water until help arrived – no mean achievement for a man whose own stubbly head scarcely topped five feet.

Back in civilian life, Major Hawkins married and settled down to a safe but dull job in an estate-agent's office. Charlie resumed his old trade of poaching and odd-jobbing. He contracted liaisons with several women, one after the other, all of whom had the good sense to clear off when their reforming zeal had exhausted itself against the immovable object of Charlie's life style.

The two old soldiers avoided each other for twenty years, but in World War Two, Major Hawkins was appointed commander of the local Home Guard. And who should appear in the ranks but Charlie.

'Oh, no,' muttered the Major as he faced another war saddled with Sloper.

This time it wasn't so bad. At least the Major saw Charlie only three or four times a week, and Charlie's nocturnal activities kept the Home Guard platoon supplied with wild game to supplement their domestic meat rations. The Major's patriotism would not allow him to buy anything on the black market – he even refused the odd bits of extra meat offered by the butcher – but he could see nothing wrong in the occasional rabbit, hare or pheasant, so long as it was legitimately come by. And for that he had Charlie's solemn oath.

(Charlie's solemn oath lost a little of its credibility over the Christmas of 1943. The goose he supplied was delicious, and Major and Mrs. Hawkins enjoyed it enormously. But after the discovery of a chronic shortage of ornamental geese on the lake of the local manor house, Charlie got a severe talking-to.)

After the war, Major Hawkins found life lacking in savour. His job was dull and not too well paid. His social-ladder-climbing wife, who had hoped for better things from him, chose their friends. So he started going into the public bar of the Tadchester Arms to renew his association with Charlie.

It had to be the public bar: Charlie was not allowed in the saloon for a dozen good reasons. Although the Major looked distinctly out of place, he quickly became very popular with the regulars as a fount of knowledge, arbiter of bets and arguments, but most of all because of the repartee between him and Charlie.

The Major played up to his officer image, greeting Charlie with 'Good morning, Sloper, you squalid little man. Gad, if the Germans had only known.'

Charlie would respond with a few bars of *Colonel Bogey*, a raspberry and a sophisticated 'Piss orf!' Then the real fun would start. For an hour they would insult each other until the air was blue.

Sometimes they would have arguments in earnest, usually after Charlie had done something anti-social such as scrumping from the Major's fruit trees, or been caught green-handed with a cabbage from Mrs. Hawkins' kitchen garden. Mostly, however, it was purely in fun. Their bonds grew even stronger after the Major's six-month illness, during which Charlie walked his dog twice a day, even though Mrs. Hawkins would allow him no nearer the house than the garden gate.

It wasn't possible to blame Mrs. Hawkins entirely: she had let him in once and he and the very sick Major had got roaring drunk on a bottle of scotch which Charlie had smuggled in. Mind you, it probably did him more good than a whole arsenal of antibiotics.

*   *   *

So the strange friendship went on: fun for everybody and especially for the two old Contemptibles. But eventually the years began to tell.

Charlie grew progressively scruffier, dirtier, smellier. His clothes, which he filched from dustbins and whatever was thrown out at the end of jumble sales, became tattier and more bizarre. A worn but well-made leather brogue on one foot, a teenager's training shoe on the other; on one hand a fur-lined gauntlet, on the other a perforated lightweight driving glove: this was nothing unusual. And in between was a collection of faded, dirty, greasy tatters which would have disgraced a scarecrow.

He seemed to have given up washing altogether. Round about Christmas time he would appear with his face a few shades lighter, but his beard remained untouched. The public bar regulars gave him plenty of room, especially when the bar warmed up.

For years bets had been laid about what colour Charlie would be underneath if he ever really washed. The nearest anybody came to knowing was when he spilled some brown ale on his hand and rubbed it against his coat. The man nearest to him swore that he had glimpsed a flash of white, but it needed corroboration before the bets could be paid . . . and by the time another witness was called, Charlie had rubbed his hand again and smeared it back to its original off-black colour.

Charlie's home, an old unsanitary cottage, was apparently very much like Charlie himself, and you entered at your peril. Fine if you didn't mind fleas, lice and bubonic plague, but not so good if you had any reservations about such things. I had no opportunity to find out: Charlie never ailed, never had done in the whole of his life, and seemingly wasn't going to start now.

As Charlie became scruffier over the years, so the Major became more fastidious. And both men became less patient with each other, each prone to fly off the handle and turn the ritual banter into something approaching the nasty.

Things came to a head one warm evening. Charlie sat in the public bar, steadily ripening. One by one the regulars shifted their seats. Finally, the corner was occupied only by Charlie and Major Hawkins.

Suddenly the Major peered intently at Charlie's beard, through the tangle of which he had spied something crawling.

'You dirty, unspeakable little man!' he bellowed. 'You've got cooties!'

'No I ain't,' protested Charlie, hurriedly wiping his beard. 'That's a drop of brown ale.'

'It's the only gravity-defying brown ale I've ever seen!' roared the Major. 'The bloody thing was walking upwards. My God, I should have had you shot when I had the chance!'

'And I should have left you in that bloody shell hole!' screeched Charlie.

That was the only mention of the shell hole either of them had ever made in public. And those were the last words they spoke to each other.

Major Hawkins stalked out of the bar, followed by raspberries and shouts of 'Piss orf!' from Charlie, and never came back to the Tadchester Arms.

A few months later the Major died. Quite suddenly, quite painlessly, and with no warning at all.

Mrs. Hawkins dealt with his death in the same brisk way she had dealt with his long illness of several years before. As soon as the death certificate was signed, she had the Major's old dog put to sleep. The funeral notices announced, 'Private ceremony. No flowers.'

Outside the lichgate of the church, as the hearse arrived, stood a little man whom nobody recognised: spruce, trim, silver-bearded, wearing a neatly pressed suit, on the breast of which hung a set of old campaign medals.

As the coffin was lifted onto the shoulders of the pallbearers, the little man sprang to attention and, ramrod straight, threw a perfectly timed and precise army salute.

'Who is that chap?' asked the manager of the estate agents', who was escorting Mrs. Hawkins at the head of the small band of mourners.

'I've really no idea,' she said.

And no more she had, until the coffin was lowered onto the trestles in front of the altar. There on the lid was a small bunch of flowers which that morning had been growing in the window box of the Tadchester Arms.

Charlie always had a way of getting round regulations. And, for once, Major Hawkins would have approved . . .

CHAPTER 12

Age and Dignity

After Alice had fully recovered from her pneumonia, I made an appointment for her to see Mr. O'Malley, specialist at Tadchester Hospital.

'O'Malley,' said Alice to her daughter Phil as she prepared for the trip. 'He sounds like a good little Catholic to me. Do you reckon he's a little Catholic, Philomena?'

'Look here, mother,' said Phil. 'It doesn't matter if he's a Bush Methodist or sitting on a bed of nails. You're going there for an examination, not Communion. Now don't you dare mention anything about religion.'

'I won't, I won't,' said Alice. 'Not a word. But it would be nice if he turned out to be a little Catholic.'

Mr. O'Malley broke the news.

'You have gallstones, Mrs. Mitchell, and a stomach ulcer. Normally I would operate, but because of your age and your breathing, I think it would be too much of a risk. Don't worry at all: just take things a bit steadier from now on.'

'Oh, thank you, Mr. O'Malley,' said Alice. 'I knew you'd find out what was wrong with me. With a name like that you had to be good.

'Tell me,' she said, before the horrified Phil could stop her, 'are you by any chance a little Catholic?'

'Little' hardly described Mr. O'Malley's sixteen stone weight and prop-forward build, but he replied, 'Yes. As a matter of fact I am.'

'Saints be praised!' Alice exclaimed. 'I knew it all along. Didn't I tell you, Philomena?'

As Phil blushed and spluttered, Alice grabbed Mr. O'Malley's hand.

'I'd just like to thank you ever so much for sorting me out. It must be a terrible job you've got, telling people what's wrong with them all day. I don't know how you stand it. The strain must be something cruel. You just make sure that you relax now and again and get plenty of sleep. And don't brood over things. You could make yourself poorly like that, you know.'

Alice left, almost frogmarched out by the embarrassed Phil. She left behind her a specialist who suddenly felt very tired, very worried and very, very sorry for himself – good little Catholic though he was.

*   *   *

Philomena Fraser visited Tadchester Hospital every week on early closing day to do the hair of the old ladies in the geriatric ward. All she charged was the cost of the materials: her own time and skills she gave for nothing.

Even though in many cases the hair was down to a few white and wispy strands, the fact that it was still worth the attention of a hairdresser raised the morale and self-respect of the old dears no end.

Phil's hairdressing sessions were the social highspot of the week. The old ladies gathered in the little room used as the salon, and sat around as if they were at Vidal Sassoon's. They read magazines as they waited, and chatted away to each other as if they had met for the first time that week.

The sessions were always full of laughter. Phil called all the 'customers' by their first names, and joked incessantly with them.

'Come on, Edie, love,' she'd say as an old dear tottered slowly to the chair. 'The rollers will be cold by the time you get here.' And, 'What do you fancy this time, darling? Something a bit more sexy? Be careful, though: you don't want to get that young doctor going, do you? You know what he's like when he sees you . . . especially with your teeth in.'

The good humour of the afternoon lasted all evening, long after Phil had packed her gear and gone home. The old ladies would be admiring each others' coiffures, recalling all the jokes and laughing at the sauciness until well after lights out.

The sessions were threatened though, after the matron dropped in on one of them. She stood in the doorway of the room, coldly observed the scene, listened to the banter for a few minutes, then left.

As Phil walked down the corridor after the session, lugging the drier and a suitcase full of equipment, she was hailed from the matron's office: 'I say, Hairdressah!'

'Yes, matron?' said Phil cheerily, dropping her gear and poking her head round the office door.

'Come in and close the door behind you, Hairdressah,' said matron. 'There's something I have to say.'

'What's up?' asked Phil, her smile fading at the look on matron's face.

'You must remember that this is a hospital, Hairdressah, not a social club or a beauty parlour. We expect certain standards of behaviour and have certain rules for the benefit of all which must be observed. I'm sure you understand.'

'No, I don't,' said Phil. 'Not a word. What are you on about?'

'Your conduct of the hairdressing sessions,' said matron. 'It puts the wrong ideas into the patients' heads. They are old ladies, not silly bits of girls. Your visits leave them chattering and giggling like flibbertigibbets and totally unamenable to discipline.

'Furthermore, I notice that you are in the habit of addressing them by their first names. This must cease. It has always been a firm rule that patients are to be addressed by their correct

133

titles: Miss or Mrs. followed by their surnames. Is that clear, Hairdressah?'

Phil stood there for a second, shocked and disbelieving, then came suddenly to the boil.

'It's perfectly clear, matron. Now I'd like to make a few things clear to you. Firstly, my name is not Hairdressah. It is Mrs. Philomena Fraser. Everybody calls me Phil, but to you, it's Mrs. Fraser.

'Secondly, I am perfectly aware that they are old ladies. And so are they; only too aware. The one thing they crave is to be young and attractive again. I can't give them back their youth and I can't make them pretty. But I can make them feel good, if it's only for one afternoon a week. You look after their bodies. The consultant geriatrician looks after their poor old minds. But I make them feel *feminine*. And at eighty-odd that must be a good thing for a woman to feel.'

'Now look here!' snapped matron.

'I've not finished yet,' said Phil. 'Thirdly, they like being

134

called by their first names: even by the nicknames they had when they were young. Miss Victoria Patience Bassington loves nothing more than to be called Buster, the name she had when she was captain of her school hockey team all those years ago. Mrs. Sarah Elizabeth Holmes was Sally as a girl; inside that old body she's still Sally.'

'I shall report your conduct and your attitude to the proper authorities,' said matron.

'Report away,' said Phil. 'Fourthly, the old loves I have sitting around the hairdressing sessions are completely different from the apathetic souls who sit around the ward all week. They relate to each other, they come alive, they're having an adventure. Above all, they're having some laughs. That may be against the rules, but in my book it's the finest tonic in the world.'

'I think it's high time . . .' said matron.

'You're right,' said Phil. 'It's high time I left. But I shall be back for next week's session and conduct it exactly as I have been doing, and shall continue until such time as I'm told to go. But remember: I'm not doing this for money, and I'm certainly not doing it for practice. I'm doing it because I love these old dears and I might just be making their last days a little more bearable.

'You must excuse me now, I have a family to look after and they'll be wanting their tea. And you have to make your report.'

The matron's report went in to the next meeting of the hospital committee. It didn't stay before them long: the committee members visited the hospital frequently and were well aware how much the old ladies enjoyed Phil's visits. They went further than just dismissing the report: they asked the consultant geriatrician to have a quiet word with the matron, pointing out the psychological benefits of the hairdressing sessions. He was glad to do it, and from then on Phil had no more trouble.

Matron never addressed her as 'Hairdressah!' again. In fact

she never addressed her at all if she could avoid it, but when she did it was, 'Mess-ezz Fraysah!'

'Really funny, that,' said Phil. 'She sounds just like Charles Laughton in *Mutiny on the Bounty*. And perhaps it's not entirely coincidence.'

*   *   *

What matron couldn't accomplish, old Nellie Raines almost did.

Nellie was within a couple of days of her ninetieth birthday, and Phil gave her a really special hairdo.

'There you are, love,' said Phil, after she had combed the last curl into place and put Nellie's spectacles on her nose so that she could see into the mirror. 'How does the birthday girl like that?'

Nellie peered into the mirror and her wrinkled old face lit up.

'It's beautiful, Phil,' she said. 'Beautiful.'

'Right, then,' said Phil, turning away to pick up a towel. 'We'll have you out of there, me old love, and get to work on the next young lady.'

When Phil turned back, Nellie was still sitting there, looking into the mirror with a blissful smile on her face.

'Come on, Nellie,' said Phil. 'We know you're beautiful, but you can't sit there all day admiring yourself. Who's next for shaving?'

Another old lady got up and hobbled towards the chair. Still Nellie didn't move.

'Nellie, darling,' said Phil. 'You'll have somebody sitting on your knee if you don't shift yourself. Let's be having you, Nellie? Oh, my God . . .'

Her eyes still open, and smiling rapturously, Nellie was stone dead.

'I nearly gave it up there and then,' Phil said to me afterwards. 'But I told myself that in a geriatric ward, this was always on the cards and it didn't seem to upset the others too much. The next old dear hobbled up, looked at Nellie, and said, "She's dead, you know. But doesn't she look lovely? So happy."

'After Nellie had been taken away, I carried on. The others were expecting it, and I knew that if I broke off then I'd never go back. Poor Nellie, missing her birthday. But the other old dear was right. She did look lovely . . . and so happy.'

CHAPTER 13

Growing Up

My children were growing up, as all children do, too quickly. Trevor had passed his eleven-plus and would be leaving the junior school that Paul still attended. It was the only school he had ever known.

The boys were quite different in temperament. Trevor was an avid reader, studious, and not athletically inclined. Paul was the extrovert, the all-round gamesman, always kitted out with the latest games equipment. Even by himself, he would not dream of knocking a cricket ball about in the garden without wearing white flannels, pads, cricket boots, batsman's gloves, a white sweater and a club cap.

Games at the junior school were limited. The school had few facilities and the curriculum allowed little time to play. The pupils, however, nearly all got through the eleven-plus.

The school did produce one outstanding sporting personality: the only truly consistent team manager that I have ever come across. She was the boys' games mistress: one Miss Polonsky. Polish, in her sixties, she wore ankle-length skirts and gym shoes, and ruled her team with a rod of iron.

She was straight 5:3:2:1 on formation. When she gave you your position on the field, this was your position for life. Each

position had its own strict geographical limitation. The goal-keeper could not cross the goal-lines; neither back could leave the penalty area; the half-backs could not cross the halfway line and had to stick to their respective parts of the field, either left, right, or centre. The forwards could not cross the halfway line, backwards, that is. They had to keep pressing ahead. If the left wing should wander over to the right, it could mean fifty lines and an hour's detention. If the centre-forward deviated anywhere from the midfield he was likely to get a rap across his kneecap with a heavy whistle.

The system resulted in Trevor, who had as much athletic grace as a young hippo, getting his only good report for sport. In the space for games were the words 'Football. Good positional player'. He was the right-back and it suited him to stand happily on one spot for the hour-and-a-half of his games afternoon. Wild horses could have dragged him out of the area – but only after a struggle.

His companion in the penalty area, the left-back, was a boy

of great ability and the star of the team. It was easy to imagine his frustration at being confined to the few yards of the penalty box. One day, with a rebellious outburst, he neatly took the ball from the foot of one of the opposing forwards in his own penalty area. As if the ball were glued to his boots, he twinkled magically through the field, beat the ten men in front of him with yards to spare, and scored a thundering goal.

The games mistress immediately ruled him offside, and his subsequent gesture (which he claimed was a victory sign but was really something very rude) resulted in his being sent off and barred from football for a fortnight.

While Trevor was at the school the football side never won a game. Nor were there records anywhere registering a win under this particular management.

Miss Polonsky had been games mistress for twenty years when the boys arrived. The school's continuing lack of goals under her leadership would qualify her as material for the *Guinness Book of Records*. As she always explained, it is taking part, not winning, that is the essence of sport. And at least her teams were consistent.

*   *   *

Having children brought us a new range of friends. The children were always going to parties, and there were picnics, and all the other usual comings and goings. This additional travelling presented new problems. It was fine when we lived Up-the-Hill as we were near public transport and walking to the town was no trouble. Since we had built our house near the river, we were a good mile-and-a-half away from the main centres of activities.

Pam longed to have a vehicle of her own, shortage of money being the only thing stopping her. One of the first things we did after building our house was to buy a boat. You could not live near the river's edge without a boat, and money spent on the boat meant no money for a car.

Kevin Bird, who had a finger in everything, solved the problem. 'A second vehicle is no problem,' he said. 'Come over to Winchcombe with me one Wednesday afternoon. I can get you something for about £30.'

I didn't believe it, but two weeks later he took me to a park behind one of the Winchcombe garages, full of derelict and rotting cars. The best and most presentable of them were a battered old Ford and a 10 cwt van. The van had a box-shaped body and a long battered bonnet, but looked in reasonable condition compared with the rest of the vehicles in the yard.

'That's the one,' said Kevin.

Knowing nothing about cars or engines, I could not contradict him and left him to do the haggling. He bought the van for £25.

We had been given a lift to the garage by one of Kevin's associates, confident that we would have something to drive back in. The journey in the old van was surprisingly uneventful. The hand brake was difficult to get off, the steering wheel did swing about a bit, and the traffic flipper indicators worked only spasmodically. But the thing did go.

We drove home to Millstone. This was the name we had given to our new house after I had finally paid all the bills, fixed up the mortgage and shuddered at the hidden extras.

I was so looking forward to seeing Pam on wheels of her own at last. I called to her from the drive, full of confidence.

141

'Surprise, surprise, darling. A cherished ambition is about to be fulfilled.'

'Oh, a car!' cried Pam, as she rushed outside to be confronted by the grey 10 cwt van. Her face dropped. Whatever she had been expecting to see, it certainly wasn't this.

'It will be useful,' she said, with a hint of sarcasm, 'for when you go net fishing.'

I couldn't deny that the thought had crossed my mind that it would be easy to stow all the fishing gear in the back.

'Anyway, providing it goes,' she said, 'I'll settle for it.'

The van was named Emily by the children and became part of the family folklore. As well as the minor defects so far encountered we found that unless you held the gear lever in place it tended to slip out of gear. Turning off roads often proved difficult. Changing down, you had to keep one hand on the gear lever. Not being able to rely on the traffic indicator, you had to stick one arm out of the window to indicate which way you were going. This left no free hand for the steering wheel, but steering with the knees isn't too difficult when you get used to it.

Emily's golden moment came when Pam was driving the children home from school. She was taking Zara's son Nicholas back home, up the steep hill to their house. As she changed gear, the lever came right out of the box on the floor. Pam stabbed at the gearbox, managed to hit a bull's eye first time, somehow changed gear, and continued on up the hill.

The interior of the van had been whitewashed by some previous owner and there was always enough residual colour to mark your clothes if you sat at the back. For seats, we had five or six sections of sawn-off logs. They were not fastened down, so whenever the van tackled too steep a gradient Emily's passengers would slide towards the back doors.

But Emily was marvellous. Pam used to cart round Jane's pram in her. She could pack a dozen children in the back for a picnic or to go swimming. With our seine nets on board, we explored beaches for twenty miles along the coast.

Frank Squires and Eric found if they sat by the back doors of the van, facing each other, locked arms and swung to and fro as if they were rowing in opposite directions, they could make Emily's tail swing from side to side. This gave nightmares to the driver (usually me) but it was always good for a few laughs at the back.

Several friends borrowed Emily to move house. She could carry all but the largest furniture and never, mechanically, let us down. She was part of the family for five years, when with great reluctance she was used in part exchange for an elderly Ford Zephyr. We saw her intermittently for several years after this, always with a pang of nostalgia.

*   *   *

Our boat, a fourteen-foot, clinker-built dinghy with an outboard motor, did not give us quite the same fun as our dear van Emily. The river estuary was tidal and our front gate was about a hundred yards up the road from the water's edge. The heavy outboard had to be carried down to the boat whenever we used it, plus oars, rowlocks, a baler. There was also a square lug sail and mast that I had had made, convinced that one day I could sail the boat. As it had no keel, however, we were never able to manage it. We could only follow the direction of the wind, and that was usually in the opposite direction to wherever we wanted to go. To go boating at all, the tide had to be right, the weather had to be right, and I had to be off duty. For the first year we used it a lot, but as the years went by we used it less and less. It became whatever the nautical term is for a white elephant. After a while, for all the use it got, it could have been renamed the *Marie Celeste*.

Syd Boon, a boatman who had a boatshed on the river's edge just below our house, used to paint and caulk it for me every year and Horace Jewell, an old sailor patient, always made sure it was shipshape.

You had two options when you took out the boat: you could go either upstream or downstream. The important thing was to come back in with the water high, otherwise you had to drag the boat and yourself over two hundred yards of instant adhesive mud. I had two pairs of wellingtons sucked from my feet at various times when I had mistimed my journey home.

I only once ever went out to sea in her. It meant a three-mile journey down river. Kevin and Frank, both experienced sailors, came with me. At the mouth of the river we were exposed to the elements and the boat bobbed up and down like a cork. The others laughed at me as I pulled on a lifejacket and took my wellingtons off. The sea was not in my blood and I didn't intend to let it get in. I was only too pleased to get home, and after that confined myself to pottering about on the river, close to home.

The highlight of the boat's life was a picnic outing arranged for one summer Saturday. We were to go in convoy with Horace Jewell's boat. He had lent us his services and his boat for the day. I was to go on ahead by car and prepare the picnic.

In my boat were Pam, Jane, Paul, Trevor, Zara, Eric and Nicholas, and a little friend of Nicholas called Teresa. In Horace's boat were Kevin and Janice Bird, Frank and Primrose Squires, Philip and Joan Gammon and their two daughters, with Horace at the helm. The weight took the boats right down to their gunwales. I saw them safely off, then jumped in my car and drove up through the town to Wally Turner's farm. Wally and his wife Molly had prepared mountains of food, including cold roast and half-cooked chickens. We drove together across the fields down to the edge of the River Tad, which wound its way through Wally's land.

I put up a tent, set out the food, and lit a fire with a barbecue roasting spit over it. As soon as the boats came into view I hastily skewered the chickens and put them on the spit over the fire as if it was I who had given them this rich golden colour rather than Molly's gas stove.

The boats arrived with all passengers safe. They had met no particular hazards on the way up; in fact they were extremely encouraged at one point when an angler rose to his feet as my boat, skippered by Eric, passed him. The angler ran along the bank, waving at the boat, with all the children waving back at him. It was only when the boat veered near to the bank that they could hear the offensive language that accompanied the waving. The angler's line was caught on the boat's rudder. He was not at all pleased.

The river voyage had sharpened everybody's appetite, and the piles of food soon started to disappear. Wally and Molly were always marvellous hosts and whatever they produced always had a high cream content. Eight-year-old Teresa was found being sick behind a bush. On close questioning she admitted to having eaten eight paper cupsful of trifle and six cream cakes.

The climax of the afternoon was the illegal use of the seine net in the river. You had to have a special licence to use a net in this part of the river. But we were amateurs and thought that it would be fun just to see if we could catch anything.

Our seine net was about eight feet wide and thirty yards long. It had a row of cork floats on the top, and lead weights keeping the bottom rope down.

We managed to straddle it across the two boats and started to row upstream. As soon as the net was fully in the water, the current in this narrower part of the river caused the boats to be dragged downstream however hard we rowed. We got to the bank with a struggle. We had kept the two ends of the net upright and somehow we all got on to the bank and began to draw the ends in.

There was tremendous excitement on the bank. The children had never seen us net fishing before – we had always done it at night on the coast.

As the net came in something startlingly white could be seen at the far end. The excitement among the kids rose to fever pitch. With one last heave the whole net was on the bank and Frank rushed forward with a stick to stun the great white fish at the end of the net.

The children crowded round. Suddenly the most hysterical laughter came from Philip, who was unfolding the net. He stood in front of it, pushing back the children who were crowding round to see our catch. I shoved past him to see what

145

was causing his merriment. Then I fell about in hysterics and helped him block the view. Our gleaming white object, our magic fish, had turned out to be a male contraceptive device whose other name is given to the correspondence you use if you have a pen pal in France.

The children were disappointed that they didn't see the catch and could not understand the hysterical laughter from the adults. But later they all voted it their best day ever.

Since then the kids have grown old enough to be told the story of the catch and to understand the adults' embarrassment.

'Full marks, dad,' said Paul several years later, stretching his six-foot-odd length on the settee. 'That's one true fishing story that's not boring. Something I'll be able to tell my grandchildren. Memories are made of this . . .'

CHAPTER 14

Schooldays

Just before I came to Tadchester, George Tonbridge had arrived with ambitions to run his own school. A teacher and educationalist with very definite ideas of his own, George started off with fifteen boys. In eleven years he had built up a boys' public school with 300 pupils.

George was a man of tremendous energy and enthusiasms. As it was his school, his money, he reckoned that he had the right to make changes of any kind at any time. As the school grew in size he would wander round, making instant, erratic and empirical decisions – that a new classroom should be built, or an old one pulled down or moved. He changed the site of the swimming pool three times altogether, twice after excavations had started, and would wander into a class and intervene with his own brand of instruction, regardless of the subject or who was teaching it.

He nearly drove his staff mad and, indeed, there was a steady turnover on the fringes. The majority, however, stayed with him. He had an infectious magic which almost always won through, and which could fill the most hesitant or timid teacher full of confidence.

It must have been this infectious magic which persuaded me

to take on the job of school medical officer: I can't think of anything else which would have made me do it. It was rewarding in many ways, but added an extra dimension of worry I could well have done without.

Many of the boys' parents were based overseas. In trying to do their best for their children from great distances, they would send demands for all sorts of unnecessary medical treatment. There would be a telegram from Brazil saying, 'UNDERSTAND JAMES BUMPED HEAD THREE WEEKS AGO stop IMPERATIVE HEAD IS X-RAYED.' Other parents were of homoeopathic bent and would leave instructions that their son must never have antibiotics or other such medicines, and that at any hint of illness he should be whipped up to London to see some chosen homoeopath or chiropractor.

I sometimes forgot, and gave James or whoever the normal treatment, earning myself virulent letters from Hong Kong or the Philippines saying I would be reported to the British Medical Association, struck off, or at the very least sorted out in some way the next time the parents were in England.

With so many boys going to so many different places at holiday times, the last month of term was always a nightmare. I had to see that each boy had the vaccinations and immunisations required for his particular destination. However many notices the school matron put on the board there would always be one or two boys turning up the day before they were about to leave school saying, 'I'm off to Chile tomorrow.' (Or Morocco or Bombay or Djakarta) 'Do I need any injections?'

I found that being school medical officer took up a disproportionate amount of my time. Not only did the job entail dealing with sick boys and anxious parents, it also meant routine medical examinations, attendance at boxing and rugby matches, sports days and speech days. Not only that, some of the teachers would regard me as their own private doctor and accost me in the common room with all sorts of real and imaginary afflictions. Being highly educated, teachers not only required medical treatment but also a detailed explanation of exactly what was going on and what effect the treatment would have. It was all rather tedious.

I tried, patiently, to explain that to understand fully what I was saying, they ought really to have had two years' anatomy and physiology and three years' clinical medicine, and a pharmacy degree on the side.

Once or twice I marched into George's study to resign. Inevitably I came out cheerful, resolute and brimming over with confidence. What George had said had really inspired me. The strange thing was that I could never remember what he *did* say.

One day I asked, 'George, how do you cope with all this – the boys, the staff, the parents, the organising, the expansion? Don't you ever feel like packing it all in?'

(This time I did remember his answer.)

'I taught maladjusted children for several years,' said George. 'It cost me my fiancée and almost my sanity before I finally quit. Compared to that, this is easy. A piece of cake.'

George's story of his time at the school for maladjusted children had me convinced that coping with this present school really *was* a piece of cake, and I felt guilty about complaining. The maladjusted children he had taught were very bright. In many cases their superior intelligence was a factor in the maladjustment.

The policy of the school was to make information on their maladjustment available to the boys, to help them come to terms with it. Naturally, they talked among themselves with the consequence that every boy in the school knew what the others' symptoms were. Sometimes they would taunt each other with their conditions: 'Yah! Soppy old Turner! Enuretic, aren't you, Turner? Old pee-the-bed! Old soggy pants.'

The boys called all the teachers, including the headmaster, by their first names. Their conversation was as frank and open as their language was colourful. And this led to the split between George and his fiancée, Hilda.

Hilda still lived in George's home town, Cheltenham, so George's appointment to the school had meant a separation. She came down in the summer for Open Day. A good-looking girl, and a natural blonde, she immediately attracted the attention of the boys.

'Hey, George!' they called. 'Nice bit of stuff you've got there. Bet she's a right goer! What's her name?'

George introduced Hilda, who was blushing madly.

'Are you and George having it away then, Hilda?' asked one of the boys.

'What's he like in bed, Hilda?' asked another.

'Never mind about George, Hilda darling,' said another, all of twelve years old. 'I can give you a much better time. See you behind the pavilion in ten minutes. Any way you like it...' And here he launched into a list of sexual techniques which would have made a sailor blush.

'George!' commanded Hilda. 'Stop this boy's filthy mouth!'

'All right, Geoff,' said George. 'Do me a favour.'

The boy stopped.

'And make him apologise!' said Hilda.

'Certainly not,' said George.

The school encouraged the boys to talk freely as part of their therapy. While they were talking they were getting things out of their systems and unconsciously providing clues about their maladjustments.

After another demand for an apology and another refusal, Hilda stormed off. That was the last George saw of her. A couple of days later she returned the engagement ring in the post.

'I was very cut up at the time,' said George. 'But it was all for the best. She'd have made a dreadful teacher's wife, even in a school where the kids were normal.'

'And was that what made you give up maladjusted teaching?' I asked.

'I'd rather you rephrased that,' George chuckled. 'God, no. It took more than Hilda. It was young Simpson. And the longest ten seconds of my life.'

He paused and gazed absently out of the window.

'Go on, for God's sake, George,' I said. 'Don't leave it there.'

'Sorry. Yes, young Simpson. About fourteen he was. Sickly,

151

asthmatic. Parents at daggers drawn. Bullying father, director of a big merchant bank, despised his son because he was physically weak. Over-protective mother. Just about all you need for a maladjustment.

'He was bright, that boy. Wipe me off the chess board in ten minutes and run rings round me at bridge. But disturbed ... he was possibly the worst case the school had had to handle.

'It was the usual things at first: breaking windows, odd bits of sabotage, provocative behaviour. All really appeals for attention; cries for help. I spent a lot of time, and so did the other staff, trying to make him see that people did care for him, did worry about him.

'But it's difficult for outsiders to replace the love which ought to come from inside the family, and his behaviour grew worse. One night he set fire to the dormitory curtains. Another time he picked up the school cat, which had wandered into the dorm, and its fur brought on an attack of asthma. The little sod did no more than throw the cat through the window, straight through the glass. The dorm was on the second floor and the poor cat broke its back.

'It was in that dorm we had the confrontation which made me realise I was not God. If I were, I think I'd resign: being God is no fun.

'I was doing the rounds at lights out when some boys came running from the top dorm. It was Simpson, they said. Out on the window ledge. Threatening to jump.

'I ran up to the dorm and there he was; out on the ledge. In his pyjamas on a bitter winter's night. I made the boys stay clear and I went to the window to try to talk him back in. The proper drill, I suppose, would have been to have called the police and fire brigade. But by the time they arrived – remember this was way out in the sticks – he would either have jumped, fallen or frozen to death.

'With every attempt I made to make him see reason, he became more and more bitter. "You're like all the rest of them," he kept saying. "No better than my bloody father. Nobody in this world gives a damn about me and I'm better off out of it!"

'Finally, after no argument had had the slightest effect on him, I decided on the most awful gamble. "All right," I said. "Jump, you little bastard. Jump!"

'He looked at me in total disbelief and I was able to hold his eyes in a battle of wills. Suddenly he burst into tears, crumpled on the ledge, and held out his arms to me. I grabbed him, yanked him in, and held him like a baby while he sobbed his heart out.

'From my challenging him to his collapsing seemed like ten years. I found out later it was exactly ten seconds.

'From that night on Simpson began to improve. Even his asthma attacks became less frequent. He realised that he had cried wolf once too often and that his bluff had been called, and better then than later in life. We became great friends, but that was the end of my work with maladjusted kids. I couldn't go through another trauma like that. At the end of the year I left to start the school here with some money from a legacy.

'So you can understand now, Bob, why this place really is a piece of cake. Now then, what was it you wanted to see me about...?'

*　　　*　　　*

A few weeks after my conversation with George, he began to have problems which confirmed very much the old saying that you can't have your cake and eat it.

The first problem was related to the screening of a television series on escapes from a prisoner-of-war camp. Boys started disappearing during the night and reappearing a hundred miles away three days later, having been living on turnips and making forced marches by night.

As most of the parents of the 'escapees' lived on the other side of the world, the Post Office made a huge profit from long-distance telephone calls and telegrams until the TV series ended and the boys gave up the habit.

Although this first problem seemed to have been solved, there were shorter-lived and inexplicable disappearances.

George was beginning to wonder if he was losing his reason.

The science block was a prefabricated, single-storey building, and out of bounds after school hours. George noticed an increasing number of boys hanging round the block outside lesson times, and on three occasions actually saw boys enter.

He rushed to the building to nail the culprits, but inside there was no trace of anyone. He looked in cupboards, under desks, but there was just no one. George even went to the optician to have his eyes checked. He had heard of people having floating bodies in their eyes: he wondered whether it was these bodies that were floating into the science block.

He admitted his fears to the head of the science department who, to George's relief, had noticed exactly the same phenomena but had not liked to say anything for fear of looking foolish.

They decided to lay a trap. The science block had two rooms and two entrances. So on a Wednesday half-day George and the science master kept watch and saw six boys go into the science block, one by one.

'We've got them this time!' said George. He rushed to cover one entrance, while the science master covered the other.

Both rooms of the building were completely empty. They had noted the names of the six boys going in, but all were present at an immediate roll call in the grounds. Definitely nobody had left the block.

One afternoon the science master smelled cigarette smoke in class. He was convinced that some boy was smoking behind his desk. No boy would admit to it so the master paraded round the room, determined to solve this crime at least.

There was no sign of any cigarette behind any desk. But over a trap door leading to the floor space below the room, he thought the smoke hung a bit more heavily than it did anywhere else. He pulled open the trap door and was met by a blaze of electric light and a dense cloud of cigarette smoke. He peered through the trap ... and saw a sheet-lined, underground cavern, lit with a string of electric light bulbs.

Lying on cushions, smoking cigarettes, with a bottle of beer each to hand, were three sixth-formers.

The guilty parties were hauled out and the whole story eventually extracted.

It was a hangover from the escaping days. The boys had found the floor space that lay under the two classrooms, with a trap door to each. A few enterprising ones had dug a connecting tunnel, perfectly shored up, to the groundsman's store shed. The mains had been tapped to produce electric light, sheets stolen to line the walls, and blankets to carpet the floor. What had started off as a hidey-hole for two or three was gradually extended. Boys who found out about it had to join the underground organisation, and in all thirty-six boys admitted belonging to it.

George laughed when he told me about it. 'The awful thing is,' he said, 'I have to punish them. I really ought to give them marks for initiative.'

The ringleaders were suspended for two weeks and the

participants were made to fill in the underground cavities and all do an extra term's work on the allotments. As George said, they were so fond of the earth he would let them have a proper go at it – in daylight.

It was reassuring to know that, if ever (God forbid) there was a future war our school had produced, among the many fine scholars and athletes, a goodly number of highly trained escapees and tunnellers,

CHAPTER 15

Writers' Summer School

Bob Barker, my bookseller friend at Sanford-on-Sea, was always encouraging me to have a go at writing. So, too, was Herbert Hodge, local taxi-driver-cum-author, who had been an extremely successful writer and broadcaster. I procrastinated. Life was very full with medicine, Round-Table activities, fishing, friends, family and the children. I was always making the excuse that I would get round to writing when I had time.

We had living in Tadchester one well-known author, Joan Courage. She had written well over thirty books and had contributed to a number of radio and television programmes. I asked her advice about writing.

'You don't go round asking people whether you should start writing or not, Bob,' she said. 'You just get down and do it. Lack of time is no excuse. I know you are a busy doctor, but what time do you get up in the morning?'

'About 7.30,' I said.

'Get up at six' said Joan. 'And write until 7.30.'

She paused just long enough to allow this to sink in, then continued, 'If you are really interested in becoming a writer I suggest that you come with Connie White and myself to the

writers' summer school in Derbyshire. You will have a week under the same roof with 350 other aspiring writers. There are courses on different aspects of writing, such as the short story, writing for radio and television, as well as celebrity lectures and a hectic social life. It lasts a week and it's inexpensive.

'Meanwhile, don't ask me again whether you should start writing. Either get on with it or be quiet about it.'

Considerably chastened I came home and discussed it with Pam. She thought that I had been working too hard and that a writers' school would provide a welcome break.

The longer I lived in Tadchester, the greater my work load had become. The number of people who depended on me for support rather than for actual straightforward medical treatment steadily increased. So many people had such horrendous lives for a whole variety of reasons. I found I was advising them to cope with situations that I felt certain I could not have coped with myself.

I knew that Steve Maxwell carried an even greater work load than I did, and I just didn't know how he managed. I sometimes felt like the man in the variety act who spins plates on the top of canes. He increases the number of plates until in the end he has about thirty spinning, and has to rush from one to the other, giving them a twist to keep them going, trying to stop any of them falling to the ground.

I told Steve and the others that I was going to a writing school, and from then on they all pulled my leg. There would be notes reading, 'Would Somerset Maugham please go and see Mrs. Brown up the hill', or 'Could Mr. Cronin spare a minute after the evening surgery.'

I felt I had to make a start by writing something before I went to the school, if only to justify my attendance there. I followed Joan's advice and got up early in the mornings, and as Bob Barker had suggested I started to write down some of my own experiences.

A patient I greatly admired was Miss Gill, a delightful elderly lady, who had made a great success of living although she had been bedridden for forty-seven years, looked after by her friend Miss Booth. She once said, 'People come to see me because I have time to listen.'

I built up a little story about her and Miss Booth and a robin that used to visit them, and how they were affected by a television set they were given. After forty-seven years the television set freed Miss Gill from her bed. For four months she was able to watch things such as a Royal wedding, church services, cricket matches and tennis matches before she quietly died.

It was when I tried to put my thoughts down on paper that I realised the depth and strength of character of these two delightful ladies. What a wonderful couple, what a marvellous story.

The other story I tried to write was about Ben Fellowes, an upholsterer with cancer of the lung who kept on asking for the date when he was going to die. He tidied up his affairs and died on the exact day that he was told he was going to.

Ben was very brave and had great natural dignity. I wrote of him: 'I only knew him in this last phase of his life, but I always felt that he was one of those few men who, spurning hope, have the rare courage to see things as they are. When he saw the problem without adornments he said to himself, "The only thing that I have left to do is to die. I will make the best job of it I can."'

159

Joan encouraged me to submit my stories to the Talks Department of the BBC. She showed me how to present the manuscripts, and I had them typed and sent them off. Joan warned me that it would be months before I heard anything from them and added that I should not be too hopeful as the chances of having one's first scripts accepted were pretty slim.

Nothing ventured, nothing gained ... and at least I had actually written something.

Eventually it was time for the writers' summer school. Connie White came down to stay for a couple of days. She was a children's writer, and one of the wisest, nicest ladies I have ever met, a sort of female Bob Barker. I was to drive Connie, Joan and myself up to the school at Swanwick in Derbyshire.

Joan was a great talker. I don't think Tadchester could offer the intellectual stimulation that she really needed. Having Connie to talk to in the car allowed her to let rip. Joan was supposed to navigate but all three of us were so engrossed in conversation that we none of us took much notice of our direction. Eventually we found that we had missed the M1. We wandered round, finding our way and losing it again as Joan got off on some other subject. Our journey to Derby took us nine hours.

The conference centre where the school was held, The Hayes, was a large old country house that had been a prisoner-of-war camp during the war. It was said that the ghosts of some of the prisoners could be seen wandering the grounds at night. It was also said, however, that one had never been seen until after the bar had closed.

The Hayes was used mainly by religious bodies for holding their annual conferences. The writers' summer school was so different from all the rest of the conferences that the staff looked forward to it. Writers were less restrained than religious delegates: certainly there is nothing on record about church elders doing an impromptu strip on the last night of conference.

The main building was a seventeenth-century mansion containing offices, various libraries and recreation rooms, with corridors leading off to numbered individual cubicles. About two hundred yards away up a hill was the main residential block, The Garden House.

The first thing that struck me when I arrived at Swanwick was the noise. Everybody was talking nineteen to the dozen. It was worse than Connie and Joan in the car. Everybody had saved up fifty-one weeks of conversation and was determined to get rid of it in this one week.

To my surprise instead of being put into one of the cubicles I was given a room near the section of the house where the celebrities, lecturers and administrators were put up. A room with my own sink and toilet next door. Much better than the cubicles I had peeped into as I walked round the building. I popped in and thanked Marjorie Harris, the secretary of the school.

'Why have I been singled out for such favour?' I asked.

'Well,' said Marjorie (and I thought she blushed), 'Joan did mention that you were a doctor. We do have the occasional accident and we hoped you wouldn't mind our calling on you.'

'Not a bit,' I said. 'Only too pleased.'

Joan had said on the way up, 'Don't tell anybody you are a doctor.' She must have forgotten that she had already told Marjorie.

Having unpacked and wandered round the grounds I went into the lecture theatre for the Chairman's welcome. As the Chairman greeted us he named various celebrities, household names in the world of writing and publishing, each of whom stood up and took a bow.

I looked on them with great awe and couldn't believe that I would be able to rub shoulders with them and talk to them. Then, to my surprise and horror, my name was called. Dr. Robert Clifford, covered with embarrassment, was introduced to the assembly. It wasn't because of any potential writing ability.

The Chairman said, 'We have with us for the first time Dr.

Robert Clifford, a budding writer. He has kindly consented to cope with any medical emergencies while he is here. Have a good look at him; he is the man you want if you are ill.'

Suddenly I began to have doubts about being a doctor amongst writers.

The meal which followed the Chairman's introduction was incredibly noisy. Everyone was shouting to be heard. I was almost hoarse by the time it had finished. Afterwards I started back to my room to sort my things out.

There were seven or eight people standing in a line on the landing where my room was situated. I walked past them, wondering what the queue was for, and went into my room. When I got inside there was a knock on the door. I opened it to meet the head of the queue.

'Are you the doctor?' he asked.

'Yes.'

'May I see you? I have a problem.'

It seemed just like home. My heart sank.

'Come in,' I said.

'Well,' said the man, 'for the past seven or eight years I have had terrible indigestion after meals and have never had the time to see a doctor. Could you give me something for it?'

I wrote a prescription for a simple antacid, and suggested as kindly as I could that coming to see a doctor on holiday wasn't perhaps the best time or place. I let him out of the door. The line of people now numbered nine or ten. I realised that I was holding an evening surgery.

The queue for evening surgery grew each day. On the evening before we left there were twenty-four people waiting for me.

After the first lecture in the evening, given by a novelist who spoke extremely well, I wandered around drinking and talking. There was no chance of getting away from medicine. Everywhere I went, people greeted me with 'Hullo, Doc.'

I found myself with a group of about half a dozen people of roughly my own age, all experienced writers. I was fascinated to hear about their writing, and they were all wanting to hear

about medicine, happily from a writing point of view. Time flew. The first time I looked at my watch I discovered that it was four a.m.

I had just got back to my room when there was a knock on the door. Marjorie Harris said, 'Could you help us please? We have a lady at the school whose husband has just died of a coronary at home. Could you come and break the news to her.'

I had to go along and see this poor lady, who the day before had left her husband for the first time ever to come to the school. He had been perfectly all right on the railway platform when she waved him goodbye, and now, less than twenty-four hours later, he was dead.

She was a highly intelligent woman and took it all extremely bravely, but she was so shattered I offered to drive her back to Canterbury the next day. She was too numb to make any decision. I gave her a sedative and said I would see her in the morning. By the morning she had come to some sort of terms with her grief, was composed and had arranged for a friend to come up from home to fetch her.

Later that morning, I attended what the curriculum described as a writers' workshop. The man conducting the proceedings suddenly stopped in the middle of his talk, and started to pull things out of his pocket and look at them intently. He seemed unaware that we were all listening to him, and I realised something was wrong. I and another delegate managed to get the meeting closed and took him to his room.

'Where am I?' he said. '*Who* am I?'

I sat in his room with him and he went on continually: 'Who am I?... Where am I?... Who am I?' He had become completely disorientated.

There was one other doctor in residence, one of the celebrity writers, who was also a vet and a host of other things. He came over and relieved me at mealtimes.

As the day wore on there was no improvement. I rang the local health authorities and they sent a man over who agreed to admit the lecturer to hospital. I then had to escort the poor chap over to the hospital in Derby, not getting back until all the day's lectures and other functions were over. I did find my group of friends from the night before tucked away in one corner of the lounge. Somehow I didn't feel tired and once again our conversation went on and on. We explored themes and ideas, and this time it was five a.m. before I got to bed.

This became the pattern of the week. The following morning in the celebrity lecture an elderly lady collapsed and I had to help carry her out to her room and resuscitate her. The days and evenings became progressively filled with medicine and the nights with my special group of friends became longer. In the end we abandoned bed altogether and would set off in a convoy of cars to have breakfast at a transport cafe a few miles outside Derby. As well as my now established evening surgery I was consulting medically most of the day. One girl who was obviously miscarrying, I sent to hospital. Two other girls thought they were pregnant. One had five or six months' obvious evidence bulking out her skirt, so I was able to give her pretty definite confirmation.

The hospital rang to say that the lecturer I had taken in two days before, was now fit. Would I collect him, and thereafterwards keep an eye on him? I was delayed in setting off: one of the elderly ladies fell and broke a hip and I had to give first aid and arrange for an ambulance.

I really was enjoying my week, in spite of it all. Sitting with my new friends at night, I had a freedom of mind that I hadn't had for many a long year. There was a highly charged and contagious atmosphere about the whole place.

I noticed the noise in the dining room was even louder than ever. We all seemed to be heading for some tremendous climax. On the last night I don't think anyone could have got any sleep at all. Nobody seemed tired and on the last morning, the Friday morning, emotions exploded. It was as if some huge and caring family were breaking up. A lot of the writers were returning to London in a fleet of hired buses and here were the most dramatic scenes of the week. Stony faced men and weeping women were watching friends and acquaintances depart. It must have been like this in the First World War when men were going back to the trenches.

I understood why. The week seemed to have been a year. My late-night group were now almost family and, in fact, I was to know them and their families for the rest of my life.

Our journey home was quiet; I think Joan and Connie had been able to get rid of every surplus word they had saved up for the last ten years. Without interruptions I was able to find all the right roads and we got home in seven hours. My eyes seemed to be glued to the windscreen. The lack of sleep, which I hadn't noticed at Swanwick, started to catch up with me.

Pam hugged me when I got back.

'What was it like having a week away from medicine?' she asked.

I smiled. 'Oh,' I said, 'there was just enough medicine to keep me going.'

I went to bed and slept solidly for forty-eight hours. I never ever tried to get completely away from medicine again.

*   *   *

Many years later, in fact, I had completely the opposite sort of experience to that at Swanwick. I opted to go on a trans-Saharan safari, and hoped desperately to be involved in medicine in foreign climes.

In the party of ten, three of us were doctors: a consultant lady gynaecologist, an American anaesthetist, and myself.

It had been my responsibility to collect the medical supplies for this venture. To be on the safe side I had got in enough to equip a medium-sized hospital. This included miniature operating sets, local and topical anaesthetics, several hundred antibiotic capsules, tablets, diarrhoea specifics, bandages, inflatable splints, suturing materials, water purifiers, anti-histamines, steroids, insulin and the usual run of dangerous drugs.

My two colleagues, not trusting anyone else to take the right stuff, had come similarly equipped, thus tripling the quantity. If we hadn't discarded some of these supplies before we left base there wouldn't have been room for us to carry petrol and water, which the other members of the party seemed to think were more important.

We three colleagues were all geared up for medical drama, although the individual objects of our expedition were quite different. Our gynaecologist was all set to do a Caesar under local; the American anaesthetist was hoping to anaesthetise for her; and I was sure I could prove myself as an expert in resuscitation of babies in desert conditions.

We had taken a brief look into the medical histories of our companions. Of the seven, four still had appendices that had not yet been removed. There was a pretty good chance that at least one would be bad.

We were due to cover about 4,000 miles of the Sahara starting from the oasis of El Golea, that marked the end of the tarmacadam road, crossing the Tadémait Plateau to Ain Salah then on to the oasis of Tamanrasset in the Hoggar Mountains; travelling south to cross the border at In Guezzam into Niger. On to stay a few days at the native market town of Agadés; then east across the dreaded Ténéré Desert to the Bilma oasis. A few days there then north back into Algeria again to the oasis of Djanet. From Djanet an expedition across the Tasilli Plateau with pack donkeys to see and photograph the rock drawings (Tasilli frescoes). Then north through Fort Polignac and the Ouargla oasis back through the oil country to El Golea, then home.

Whatever the achievements of other trans-Saharan safaris, our claim must be that we were the healthiest. In the whole six-week journey, under a merciless sun, nobody was ill. We didn't even have a case of diarrhoea. Undismayed, we sought all the time to practise our skill on the local populace.

In the Hoggar Mountains at Assekrem near the hermitage of the famous French priest Charles Foucould, my two colleagues each pulled a tooth from the mouth of a wandering Arab woman when I wasn't looking. I inspected their handiwork later. The extractions couldn't have been too difficult – I'm certain that if the patient had sneezed she would have lost her complete set without any outside help.

We were getting depressed that nobody wanted us, desperate to be needed, and the three of us used to sit in one corner of the encampment speculating on the hopefully deteriorating health of our companions.

In Agadés in Niger the anaesthetist had an asthma attack which I managed to treat before the gynaecologist got to him. In Djanet in Southern Algeria the gynaecologist had to powder my athlete's foot. In the middle of the Ténéré Desert I had to remove a foreign body from her eye and wash it out afterwards. She wasn't so pleased when I said I would be claiming to be the first general practitioner ever to irrigate a lady gynaecologist in the middle of the desert.

At the Bilma oasis we saw a mosquito and made our presence felt by insisting that the camp site be moved thirty yards from the water and that everybody took anti-malarial drugs. I was the only person to be bitten and was so full of anti-everything that any mosquito sampling me would never make it home to base.

Climbing up to the Tasilli Plateau, the anaesthetist in-

167

sisted on giving the guide two aspirins for a pain in the leg, when in fact he was only trying to tell us to go in a different direction.

We continued to look hopefully for signs of illness amongst the natives, but like members of the expedition they all looked disgustingly healthy. Before we realised it six weeks had slipped by and we were back at our base ready to fly home to England with our stores intact.

When I commiserated with my colleagues about our lack of opportunities for practising our skills, the gynaecologist told us in a snooty tone that for the last three or four evenings she had been paring the corns of the expedition leader. This was the meanest betrayal of medical ethics: knowing that he would require more than one treatment, she could have at least shared the duties.

The final ignominy was on returning to England, where I was summonsed by the Customs people for taking dangerous drugs out of the country without an export licence.

Long before the Saharan trip I had realised that you could never really get completely away from medicine. Once a doctor always a doctor. But it seemed that whenever you were trying to make an impression, you usually had to do it in competition with several of your colleagues.

A friend of mine, a doctor of philosophy, was once on a coach tour of the Nile Valley. One of the passengers was a beautiful and well-known actress. Getting off the coach one day she stumbled and hurt her ankle. She sat at the side of the road, clutching her ankle and sobbing with pain. The courier rushed back to the bus.

'Is there a doctor on board?' he asked.

My friend the doctor of philosophy rushed to help, but was beaten to the patient by a doctor of theology.

CHAPTER 16

More Things in Heaven and Earth

I do not believe in ghosts. I dare not and must not.

As a physician my function is to care for the body and, as an optional extra, the mind. As a matter of routine I am called upon to issue a death certificate, to confirm the obvious – that this body is a dead one – and to give my opinion on the cause of death.

In other and more harrowing cases, I am called in as part of a team to decide whether life, real life, is extinct. A young motorcyclist in collision with a lorry, for instance, may have a heart which is still beating, but his brain, which controls and governs the working of the rest of the body, perhaps damaged beyond repair.

The end of life is the point at which I have to set my limits as an adjudicator. Were I to worry about whether there is life after death, the whole of my own working life could very soon become insupportable.

I think about it, of course, and perhaps make one or two private admissions to myself; but if I am to do my job, it must be here ... on earth ... with the living. Once someone has crossed the border between life and death, then he or she is out of my care and hopefully in better hands.

*　　*　　*

Having got that off my chest, I can feel free to talk about the Tadchester ghosts. There were a lot of them about, as there are in every town and village in Britain with any kind of character or history. The manor house at Altriston was reputedly haunted by two ghosts; the statutory White Lady, said to be an ancestor of the Tyster family, and a priest to whom something nasty had happened during the Reformation.

Almost every old pub in the town had a ghost, though their credibility was more than open to question. The pub ghosts tended to be seen around closing time by customers whose objectivity and accuracy of observation – not to say ability to focus – were not at their best. Whenever a pub changed hands it was almost routine for the new landlord or his wife to claim to have seen the resident ghost.

'Great for business,' said Geoff Emsworth, landlord of the

Tadchester Arms, whenever another sighting was made in a local pub.

The Tadchester Arms itself had the most famous ghost; that of Henry VIII himself, who was supposed to have slept there during a peasant-bashing expedition in the West Country. And one night after hours he was seen in a dark corridor near the dining room above the pub by two new and subsequently terrified Chinese waiters.

The story received front-page treatment in the *Tadchester Echo*. It was accompanied by a photograph of the waiters, who were by now looking far from inscrutable, under the portrait of Bluff King Hal which hung in the dining room. For weeks afterwards the pub was thronged with people hoping to see the ghost.

It wasn't until much later that I discovered the truth. I was fishing with John Denton one evening. As he walked towards me along the bank, his back to the setting sun, I was looking at the silhouette of a big man wearing a rounded hat and a short cape, arms akimbo and with a straddle-legged walk: John in his pork-pie hat, open tweed jacket and wellington boots, with his thumbs tucked into his belt. The living image of the portrait in the pub. At least, to misquote W.S. Gilbert, 'In the dark with the light behind him.'

'My God, John,' I said. 'Anybody would take you for Henry VIII in that get-up.'

'Aye, lad,' he said. 'What do you think those Chinese lads saw? I'd been having one for the road with Geoff in his rooms after hours and I was letting myself out by the back stairs. You've never seen two blokes shift so fast in all your life. Not a word to anybody mind.'

'Naturally,' I said. 'But surely Geoff knew?'

'Of course he knew,' said John. 'I went back and told him. But he'd be daft to pass up a chance like that, wouldn't he? It's what he'd always said about the ghosts in other pubs – great for business . . .'

*　　*　　*

The Tadchester Arms' 'ghost' was all too solid. But a few weeks later I had a case which called for a less prosaic explanation.

Four-year-old Emma was brought to the surgery by her mother because of what she saw, or thought she saw, in her bedroom at night.

'Tell the nice doctor what you see, Emma,' said her mother.

'A kind grandma,' said Emma. 'She smiles at me and looks after me in the dark.'

She stopped. There was a faraway look in her eyes as if she were enjoying some very pleasant and private memory.

'I shouldn't worry,' I said to the mother. 'Children of this age often invent imaginary companions.'

'I don't think she invented this one,' said the mother. Then, to Emma, 'Tell us more about the kind grandma, love'.

'Well,' said Emma, 'she's ever so kind and ever so nice. Her dress has lovely ruffles around her neck. She wears a big badge in the middle of the ruffles. And she has these funny glasses on a stick.'

173

Emma went off into her trance again, a look of complete contentment on her face.

'Now, Doctor,' whispered the mother, 'both Emma's grandmothers are alive. Neither of them is as old as this lady sounds, and certainly neither of them dresses like she does.

'But an old lady – Miss Lingard – used to live in our house before us. I've asked neighbours who knew her and they all come up with the description of a kindly but eccentric spinster, who loved children, and who always dressed in Edwardian-style clothes.

'See what I'm getting at, Doctor? Every neighbour described her in the same way: wearing a high-necked dress with a lace ruff around the neck, a big cameo brooch pinned to the ruff, and using a lorgnette instead of conventional spectacles. It's Miss Lingard, Doctor, I'm sure!'

This really was a new one on me. At medical school they had mentioned nothing about spectral spinsters in out-of-date costumes. But the mother needed something to set her mind at rest.

'Emma is not distressed by the appearances?' I asked.

'On the contrary,' said her mother. 'She enjoys them, even looks forward to them. I'm sure she feels the old lady is protecting her in some way. It's just that, to me, it's so eerie.'

'The wisest course,' I said in my most convincing tone, 'would be to treat these appearances, whether they are actual appearances or just in Emma's imagination, as completely normal. When Emma mentions the old lady, show the same interest you would in an imaginary playmate.

'Make sure that she really is tired when she goes to bed, and give her a hot milk drink to help her sleep. I think you'll find that with time, as Emma develops more and more interests, these appearances will become fewer and in the end cease altogether. But please come back if there are any other developments.'

Not bad, I thought, for a piece of off-the-cuff, top-of-the-head prognosis and reassurance. But it seemed the right thing to say. I only hoped it would work.

It did. Twelve months later, the mother was in my surgery again and I asked about Emma.

'Goodness,' said the mother. 'I'd almost forgotten. Yes, it worked out just as you said it would, Doctor. The appearances did become fewer. And there hasn't been a single one since Emma started play school, nearly three months ago. It was obviously all her imagination.'

'Of course,' I said. And meant it. I had to.

*   *   *

After Emma, I began asking friends if they had had any first-hand metaphysical experiences. I was surprised by the answers. A good half seemed to have had a weird experience of some kind or other. And a good half of them, like myself, didn't believe at all in ghosts.

A similar story to Emma's was that of a younger child, again a girl, daughter of friends and just coming up to three years old.

Tracy told her parents, Les and Dolly, about the 'big genkelum' who used to sit on a chair by the bed at nights. He had 'shiny white hair', was a 'happy genkelum' and had 'one toof gone'.

'I went cold when I heard,' Les told me. 'Tracy's bedroom used to be my father's when he lived with us. He died four years before Tracy was born. He was a big jolly chap, about eighteen stone, with silver hair. He died early in the New Year. Not long before, at Christmas, he'd bitten hard on a piece of pork crackling and lost a front tooth from his top set.'

*   *   *

Harry Walters, a sceptic if ever there was one, told of his mother living with them before she died.

'She had an obsession about the drain at the back of the garage,' he said. 'She was convinced there was something wrong with it and was forever pouring bleach and disinfectant down. To keep her happy, I had men in to look at it, but they could find nothing wrong.

'Six months after her death I was planing some wood in the

175

garage, late on in the evening, when I sensed something outside. Through the window I could see my mother, peering at the drain and looking very worried. As it grew darker, she faded. I ran back into the house, telling myself it was nothing but imagination.

'But a few weeks later the drain cracked. A root from a large tree next door had forced its way into a joint and smashed a complete length of pipe from end to end. From the size of the root, it must have been in there for years. The ground subsided and the whole back wall of the garage fell down. I've felt ever since that my mother had come back to try to warn me.'

* * *

Lucy Parker told me about the birth of her son in St. Mary's Maternity Home. It was to be a breech birth – the baby was presented backside-first instead of head-first – and such births are never easy. Several attempts were made in the last few weeks of pregnancy to turn the baby in the womb, but the baby always turned back again.

'That must have been worrying for you,' I said.

'It was,' said Lucy. 'Until I woke up after falling asleep between pains. Standing by my bed was my cousin Eric, in his RAF uniform. Eric was ten years older than me, orphaned, and my mother had brought him up. He always looked upon me as his kid sister. I looked upon him as my wise, protective, big brother.

'Anyway, there he was, standing by the bed. "Don't worry, kid," he said. "Everything's going to be all right."

'I felt so peaceful then, and went straight back to sleep. The next time I woke the contractions were coming really strong, and my son was born within the hour perfectly healthy.'

'That must have been a great relief,' I said. 'I bet Eric was pleased for you too.'

'I'm sure he was,' said Lucy. 'But I've no way of knowing. He was killed during the war, flying with Bomber Command, when I was only ten.'

* * *

After all these stories I was beginning to feel a bit punch-drunk. (Can you get ghost-drunk?) So I was very pleased to bump into John Denton in the High Street.

'It's nice to meet somebody who doesn't believe in ghosts,' I said. 'Even though he does do a very good imitation of one.'

'Ghosts?' said John. 'A lot of it's in the mind. I get half a dozen reports a year of the Phantom Angler, seen at dusk by the river and vanishes when anybody gets near him. That's no more of a ghost than I am: it's that tatty little villain Charlie Sloper, knocking off my trout again.

'No, I don't believe in ghosts. But then I don't believe in total abstinence and that doesn't stop it existing in some quarters. Have I ever told you about the goings-on at my cottage?'

'No,' I said. 'But I've a feeling you're about to.'

'Dead right,' said John. 'Well, you know the place. Used to be a gamekeeper's cottage-cum-lodge. Bigger than average and with a cellar, which is unusual for cottages in these parts, but the cellar was for the keeper to hang the game in away from the gentry's sensitive nostrils, and to keep his traps and gear in.

'In the middle of the night, about three weeks after I'd moved in, I heard a dog padding up the stairs. It nosed the door open, jumped onto the bottom of my bed, and curled itself round to sleep.

'I shouted, "Our Biddy! Get back down there!" and kicked out. My foot connected with nothing: the weight at the bottom of the bed just disappeared. I switched on the light and there was no sign of any dog.

'Biddy, my collie, always sleeps in the kitchen with the door on the catch, and I was puzzled about how she'd got upstairs. So I went down. There was the kitchen door, still on the catch. I opened it, and Biddy was in her basket, inside.

'This happened several times after that. It was always the same: the sound of a dog padding upstairs, the bedroom door being nosed open, and the weight at the bottom of the bed.

'I thought, "Bloody hell! It comes to something when you're being haunted by a flaming dog. Other people get Anne

177

Boleyn." And after that I just took no notice of it.'

'Is it still happening?' I asked.

'No,' said John. 'Not the dog. That's stopped. Now I'm getting the Phantom Burglar.'

'Go on,' I said.

'Try and stop me,' said John. 'Keep all this to yourself, mind. I don't want folk round here thinking I'm barmy.'

'Scout's honour,' I said.

'Right,' said John. 'Shortly after the dog stopped coming, I was sitting in the living room having a quiet read and a glass of scotch. About eleven o'clock at night, it'd be.

'All of a sudden there was a hell of a crash from the cellar as if the window had been kicked in. There were quiet footsteps across the cellar floor. And then they started coming slowly up the steps.

'I picked up the poker and went into the kitchen to the cellar door. The amazing thing was Biddy. She's a gentle old bitch, or rather a gentle young bitch, but she's normally frightened of nothing.

'This time she was terrified. She crouched on the floor, staring at the cellar door. All the hairs on her back were up, she was trembling all over and whimpering with fright. And the footsteps kept on coming until they stopped at the top of the stairs.

'"Right, yer bugger," I thought. "I'll have you now and no messing."

'You know the light to the cellar is on the kitchen wall by the door, to stop you going arse-over-tip down the steps in the dark? Well, I switched that on with one hand, knocked up the door sneck with the poker, and charged through the door and down the steps.

'I finished up at the bottom, swinging the poker like a lunatic – and there was not a soul in sight. Not a sausage. The window was as it always is: bolted on the inside. Biddy was still whimpering at the top of the stairs. I called her down, but she wouldn't budge.

'Well, at that, I started shaking. I went back upstairs, locked

178

the cellar door, and knocked hell out of the scotch. I'm getting used to the footsteps now. It's happened three times since, all to the same pattern and all with the same results. But I've felt a bit better about it since I found out the likely cause.'

'And what's that, John?' I asked. By now we were approaching the Tadchester Arms.

'Told you I didn't believe in total abstinence, didn't I?' said John. 'With all this talking it's beginning to feel as if I'm suffering from it. And in case you think I'm completely round the bend, I'd like you to hear a bit of local history from one of our local relics. We'll find him in the public bar, I shouldn't wonder . . . After you.'

I preceded John into the public bar and ordered two pints of bitter.

'Make it three, if you wouldn't mind, Bob,' said John. 'I've found what we're looking for and it's usually thirsty. I'll see to the next round.'

John lumbered over to a corner table.

'Ah, Charlie!' boomed John.

Charlie it was. Charlie Sloper.

'Word in your ear, if I may!'

'T'warn't me,!' shouted Charlie, with a sudden appearance of panic. 'I was nowhere near your stockponds last Wednesday!'

'So that's where they went . . .' muttered John to himself. Then, 'No, Charlie. This is more of a social call. This is Dr. Clifford, who's dying to meet you and who has just bought you this pint.'

'Don't want no truck wi' doctors!' snapped Charlie. 'Never use 'em! Don't know what they're up to, most of 'em!'

'Dr. Clifford is interested in local history,' John continued, patiently. 'I'd like you to tell him about Keeper Brand.'

'Keeper Brand!' spat Charlie. 'Bastard! Shot the arse out o' my britches many a time when I was a lad. And he killed my mate! You ought to know, anyway, Bailie. You lives in his old cottage. And I told you all about him a few months back.'

'So you did,' said John. 'But you tell it much better. Go on.'

'Brand,' said Charlie, a fierce hatred in his eyes, 'was gamekeeper when all that land by the river belonged to the big estate. This is going back some. Before the Great War.

'Brand was a holy terror. Black Jack Brand we used to call him. Got so nobody could come by a pheasant or a hare or a brace of trout without getting two barrels of shot up his arse. Sit up all night by those bleeding pheasants, he would. Shotgun across his knees. And still be awake all next day. Wasn't human, if you ask me.

'He used to live in your cottage. And that's how my mate Stokie got killed. Only eighteen he were, and a good-hearted lad. Anyway, one night he sees the cottage all in darkness and he reckoned Brand was out sitting shotgun somewhere. So he got into the cellar, just to have a look around like, in case there was any game hanging up and going begging.

'The cellar was empty, so he decided to go upstairs and see what was in the kitchen. When he got to the top of the stairs, Brand was waiting for him. He must have been sitting in the cottage without lights.

'The old bastard slammed the cellar door open and knocked Stokie from top to bottom of the stairs. Smashed his skull, it did. Killed him stone dead.

'When Brand seen Stokie was dead, did he feel sorry for him? Did he buggery. First thing he did was look round for his old dog, which should have been in the kitchen. He found the dog upstairs, sleeping on his bed.

'He did no more than pick up the big ash stick he kept by his bed and beat the old dog's head in. That was Brand for you. In temper he was a madman.

'He got away with it, of course. Death by misadventure, the coroner said about Stokie. In the course of a felony, or some such rubbish. Nobody knew about the dog until Brand was in his cups here one night and let it slip.

'The old bastard was found drowned about six months after in a flash flood. Accidental death, that was. But some of Stokie's relatives could have told you different...'

'Thank you, Charlie,' said John. 'That deserves another

pint. But would you excuse the doctor and myself if we stood at the bar? We have some medical business to discuss.'

'Stand where you like,' said Charlie. 'So long as you don't forget that there pint.'

'That's better,' said John at the bar. 'I don't like sitting near Charlie too long. Apart from the pong, you're liable to pick up a few unidentified flying objects.

'Now then. See what I mean? What happened at the cottage way back could explain the dog on the bed and the footsteps in the cellar. *And* the state that Biddy gets in.'

'What about Brand?' I asked. 'Hasn't he turned up yet?'

'No,' said John. 'But I think he'd know that the cottage isn't big enough for both of us.'

'Hey,' I said. 'You're the one that doesn't believe in all this stuff.'

'Right,' said John, grinning. 'I'm an atheist, thank God. And I've never had need of superstition, touch wood.'

He winked.

'A bit like yourself, I reckon.'

*   *   *

My mother's brother, Uncle Bertie, told me of the time he heard ghosts talking in the downstairs sitting room, one winter's night in 1932.

'I was terrified,' he said. 'I was in bed and was tempted to put my head under the clothes. But I said to myself, "No I must go down and face them." It was the bravest thing I ever did.'

'I slipped on my trousers and crept silently across the landing, then started to come slowly down the stairs.

'Suddenly I heard soft footsteps behind me. Each stair I moved down, I was followed by two soft footsteps. If I stood still, they stood still. They started again as soon as I moved. These weren't the footsteps of people – they were the soft light sounds of someone from another world. The house was obviously full of ghosts, upstairs and downstairs.

'I got down the stairs at last and started to walk towards the sitting room. The footsteps stopped. Whatever it was behind me had decided to stay on the stairs to cut off my retreat.

'I was in a cold sweat but still determined. I took a lunge at the sitting-room door, pushed it open and burst in the room shouting, "Go away ghosts!"

'But there was nothing there, nothing other than the wireless that had been left switched on.'

'Oh, come on,' I said. 'Whyever didn't you think it was the wireless in the first place?'

'Well,' said Uncle Bertie, 'in those days the radio programmes closed down at 10.30 at night. What I had heard was a test transmission that they sometimes did during the night when all programmes had finished, and all radios presumably had been turned off.'

'What about the footsteps?' I asked. 'Were they just imagination?'

'No,' said Uncle Bertie. 'When I pulled my trousers on, I had forgotten to do up my braces – and the soft footsteps I heard were my braces dropping down the stairs behind me.'

TESTING
...TESTING...
WHAIL...MOAN...
RATTLE...
GROAN...

CHAPTER 17

But Once a Year

Tadchester's Christmas festivities always brought with them such a crop of bizarre accidents that I dreaded being on call over the holiday period.

Some of the accidents were caused by practical jokes.

One Christmas Eve a gang of navvies were working on a hole in a quiet road on the outskirts of Tadchester. Their lunchtime break was long and convivial.

When they got back to the hole, the largest of them – name of O'Reilly, would you believe? – was in no mood for work. He was in no state for it, come to that, and sat on an upturned barrow swigging heartily from a bottle of Bushmill's and singing lugubriously of his homeland.

When the gang were within half an hour of finishing, O'Reilly passed out. His mates decided on a jolly Christmas jape. They propped him up so he was sitting on the shallow trench in the road, put his feet in the trench and poured quick-setting cement around his wellingtons. They covered him with a tarpaulin, set the red warning lamps around the trench, and went happily home.

A policeman, attracted by muffled snores from under the tarpaulin, found O'Reilly at ten o'clock that night. Set solid. It wouldn't have been so bad if just the wellingtons had been encased: O'Reilly could have been hauled free, leaving his footwear behind. But his weight had caused his legs to sink deeper and deeper into the concrete until eventually it had oozed over the top and filled his wellingtons. When I got there his lower legs were trapped immovably.

A telephone call to the home of the contractor resulted in a scratch squad of navvies being rounded up. With the help of drills, sledgehammers, spades and picks, they eventually hacked O'Reilly free of the trench, but still with his legs in a block of concrete. The more delicate job of chipping through to the wellingtons, the socks, and the final painful prising off of the hairs on the legs, was done in the fire station where the light was better.

O'Reilly, shocked, chilled, bruised and horribly hung-over, had to spend the night under observation in Tadchester Hospital. He discharged himself on Christmas morning, lurching off in a pair of borrowed wellies and swearing every kind of slow and painful revenge on his mates. Whatever mayhem he caused must have happened outside the hospital catchment area, otherwise the Tadchester casualty ward would have been very crowded over Christmas.

'I suppose,' I said, when the hospital reported no repercussions, 'that we must be thankful for small murphies.'

*   *   *

Practical jokes like the one played on O'Reilly may sound funny, but they do have a habit of misfiring. Something similar had happened just before Christmas the previous year, when a party of lunchtime revellers had left one of their number unconscious, his arms folded across his chest, on top of a catafalque in Tadchester cemetery.

He might very well have died of exposure if he had not been discovered towards dusk by a little old lady who had gone to place some flowers on her husband's grave. As it was, he recovered quickly, but the old lady had to be sedated for shock at the discovery of what she thought was a disinterred body. After that she visited the cemetery only in broad daylight.

* * *

Even cosy family gatherings can end in catastrophe. I was called out at two o'clock one Boxing Day morning to a really big case, big because the casualty weighed twenty stone.

After shifting three bottles of scotch during Christmas night and the early hours of Boxing Day, he had lurched upstairs to bed. Halfway up he had collapsed and become wedged between the wall and the banisters. Moreover, he had started a severe nosebleed: what seemed to be pints of blood were running stickily down the stairs when I arrived.

I was greeted by four female relatives.

'We tried to shift him, Doctor,' they said agitatedly. 'But he was much too heavy.'

'Pity,' I said as I tugged at the giant frame to attempt emergency treatment, 'that there weren't any other men in the house.'

'Oh, there were,' said one of the women. 'And there still are: four of them.' She opened the door to the sitting room to reveal four comatose forms. 'All unconscious.'

The scotch really had gone the rounds that night.

* * *

Even the best-run festive occasions can go awry. In my younger days as a House Surgeon in a London hospital I used to dread hospital Christmas parties. To avoid giving offence, I would have to take a drink with every head of department, every matron and every ward sister. Apart from that there was usually some embarrassing moment for somebody. Towards the end of the jollifications, pent-up passions among the nurses would suddenly become un-pent, and some of the younger doctors were lucky to escape with their lives, let alone their trousers. The young doctors, too, were not always models of decorum. More than one would demonstrate during the evening that his interest in female anatomy was not purely professional.

185

Most of the embarrassment one Christmas came from the managing director of the firm next door to the hospital. He had got himself invited on the strength of being the friendly chap next door and on the promise of bringing vast amounts of booze.

He kept that promise all right: there were bottles and bottles of spirits and wine, and crates and cans of beer, stout and lager.

My premonition that something would go wrong became stronger as the evening wore on. The captain of industry became more and more under the influence, dancing about madly and holding the nurses in places never recommended by any school of dancing.

Finally, after a nurse's pretty dimpled knee had caught him in a sensitive spot and left him with a pained expression, it was tactfully suggested that perhaps it was time he went home to his ever-loving.

'Certainly,' he said, through clenched teeth, his eyes still watering. 'Don't bother. I can find my own way out.'

Next morning, one of the cleaners tried to use the back service lift to take the rubbish away, and found it jammed between floors. Maintenance men were called, the lift winched up and the doors opened.

There, on the floor of the lift, in a crumpled and unconscious heap, lay the captain of industry. As it turned out later, he'd got into the wrong lift, pressed several wrong buttons and then, in an attempt to hit the one for the ground floor, had connected with the emergency stop and then passed out.

The maintenance men picked him up, brought him round, and set him on his woozy way home.

'My God,' he muttered, as realisation dawned that it was now well into the next day. 'How am I going to explain *this* to the wife?'

* * *

'Soon be Christmas,' said Pam cheerily, as she made out lists for cards and presents.

Really, I love Christmas and always have done, and I loved

it especially at this time when the children took so much delight in the magic of it all. Jane would be nearly three this Christmas, and for the first time would be able to join in all the fun.

However, I could not share Pam's enthusiasm, I had the distinct feeling that this was going to be one of *those* Christmases. There was an omen.

The Tadchester Drama Society had been hard at rehearsals for its panto. This year it was to be *Dick Whittington*, with Pam in the title role.

To advertise it, a gigantic banner had been strung across the High Street, between the upper floors of the bank and the Co-op. It read:

Tadchester Drama Society proudly present
DICK WHITTINGTON
A spectacular pantomime for all the family
with
PAM CLIFFORD   KEVIN BIRD   ZARA MARTIN
The Tadchester Orpheus Choir

I was in the bank one windy morning about a week before the panto's opening, when from outside came a screech of brakes and an ominous *crump*! I ran outside to find a car with its bonnet concertina'd against a lamp post. Draped over the windscreen was the banner: the wind must have loosened the fastenings and brought it down.

The driver was dazed, had a few scratches about the head, but otherwise was intact. I helped him out and guided him into the bank, where I sat him down and checked over his cuts and bruises.

'What the hell was it?' he asked. 'All of a sudden some damn great thing flopped down onto the windscreen and I was blinded.'

'Not to worry,' I said. 'No harm done ... er ... except to yourself and the car.'

'Thanks,' he said. 'But what *was* it?'

'A banner,' I said, 'advertising the Tadchester Drama

Society's panto. It should be very good: my wife's playing the lead.

LET ME THROUGH, I'M A TICKET AGENT!

'I don't suppose,' I said hesitantly, 'that I could interest you in any tickets . . .'

My visit to the bank had not been a very happy one. The manager had called me in informally to point out the poor health of my bank account. He suggested that I should try and find some way to resuscitate it.

The outlook was bleak.

From the bank I went to see a patient who was extremely rude to me. Normally I can take rudeness especially from old or anxious patients. But this patient was neither, and the rudeness got right to me.

It was turning into a disastrous day; nothing was going right. When I got back to the surgery there was a message from Gladys, 'Will you please ring home, Dr Bob. Mrs Clifford wants you.'

Gladys looked anxious.

I rang, more than a bit apprehensive. Pam answered.

'Could you come home as soon as possible? I've some news for you that I don't want to tell you in the surgery.'

My heart sank. This was the last straw of this awful day. I had to sit through surgery, my mind racing through all the dreadful possibilities. Was my mother ill? Had some disaster befallen the children? No, if it had been a medical disaster I would have heard of it. I got out of the surgery as soon as I could.

'You got through them like greased lightning tonight,' said Grace. 'What's up with you, Dr. Bob? Have you got hot pants or something?'

'Possibly,' I said, in an attempt to keep up the banter I was in no mood for.

By the time I got home my heart was sinking lower and lower. I put the car away and dragged my feet up the steps to the front door. Pam was waiting inside.

'Look!' she called, excitedly, waving an envelope with a bit of red in one corner. 'It's from the BBC!'

'This is all I need,' I thought. 'A rejection slip.'

The BBC had had my two scripts. One about Miss Gill and Miss Booth, and one about Ben Fellowes, the man who knew he was going to die, for more than three months now. And now they were being turned down.

I unfolded the letter and read:

Dear Dr Clifford,

Many thanks for your manuscripts which we have been considering. I am happy to say that we like both these short stories and would like you to come and record them at some mutually convenient date. We are at present looking for a doctor to do some other pieces for us, and may be able to offer you a regular monthly spot if you are interested. Please ring me on extension 725.

Great! Who said it was a lousy day? This was the best day of the year. The first two things I had ever written had been accepted by the BBC. The story of Miss Gill and Miss Booth would be heard in thousands and possibly millions of homes. The courage of Ben Fellowes would get the recognition it deserved. On top of that it looked as if I was going to be able to do something creative outside medicine; something that could enlarge my medical experience, yet not interfere with my home life, the practice, or my patients in Tadchester.

I was going to be able to set off in a different direction.

Life was going to be different from now on.

As I put the letter down, my mind racing with the excitement of all the possibilities stretching ahead of me, there was a knock on the door.

I answered it. Outside stood a man in overalls, blood pouring from his hand.

'Are you the doctor?' he asked.

'Yes,' I replied.

'Sorry to bother you, sir. I was just down the road when my windscreen shattered. I punched it out and I think I got some glass in my hand.'

'Come in,' I said. 'I'll see what I can do.'

I smiled to myself.

No, life was not going to be different from now on. It was really always going to continue in very much the same way.

Postscript

There is the fable of the old man sitting outside a town, being approached by a stranger.

'What are they like in this town?' asked the stranger.

'What were they like in your last town?' replied the old man.

'They were delightful people. I was very happy there. They were kind, generous and would always help you in trouble.'

'You will find them very much like that in this town.'

The old man was approached by another stranger.

'What are the people like in this town?' asked the second stranger.

'What were they like in your last town?' replied the old man.

'It was an awful place. They were mean, unkind and nobody would ever help anybody.'

'I am afraid you will find it very much the same here,' said the old man.

If it should be your lot to ever visit Tadchester, this is how you will find us.

A selection of bestsellers from SPHERE

FICTION

JUBILEE: THE POPPY CHRONICLES 1	Claire Rayner	£3.50 ☐
DAUGHTERS	Suzanne Goodwin	£3.50 ☐
REDCOAT	Bernard Cornwell	£3.50 ☐
WHEN DREAMS COME TRUE	Emma Blair	£3.50 ☐
THE LEGACY OF HEOROT	Niven/Pournelle/Barnes	£3.50 ☐

FILM AND TV TIE-IN

BUSTER	Colin Shindler	£2.99 ☐
COMING TOGETHER	Alexandra Hine	£2.99 ☐
RUN FOR YOUR LIFE	Stuart Collins	£2.99 ☐
BLACK FOREST CLINIC	Peter Heim	£2.99 ☐
INTIMATE CONTACT	Jacqueline Osborne	£2.50 ☐

NON-FICTION

BARE-FACED MESSIAH	Russell Miller	£3.99 ☐
THE COCHIN CONNECTION	Alison and Brian Milgate	£3.50 ☐
HOWARD & MASCHLER ON FOOD	Elizabeth Jane Howard and Fay Maschler	£3.99 ☐
FISH	Robyn Wilson	£2.50 ☐
THE SACRED VIRGIN AND THE HOLY WHORE	Anthony Harris	£3.50 ☐

All Sphere books are available at your local bookshop or newsagent, or can be ordered direct from the publisher. Just tick the titles you want and fill in the form below.

Name _____

Address _____

_____

Write to Sphere Books, Cash Sales Department, P.O. Box 11, Falmouth, Cornwall TR10 9EN

Please enclose a cheque or postal order to the value of the cover price plus:

UK: 60p for the first book, 25p for the second book and 15p for each additional book ordered to a maximum charge of £1.90.

OVERSEAS & EIRE: £1.25 for the first book, 75p for the second book and 28p for each subsequent title ordered.

BFPO: 60p for the first book, 25p for the second book plus 15p per copy for the next 7 books, thereafter 9p per book.

Sphere Books reserve the right to show new retail prices on covers which may differ from those previously advertised in the text elsewhere, and to increase postal rates in accordance with the P.O.